PRACTICAL STRATEGIES

for Supporting Young Learners with Autism Spectrum Disorder

Tricia H. Shelton, EdD

with Mary Renck Jalongo, PhD

Gryphon House
www.gryphonhouse.com

Published by Gryphon House, Inc.
P. O. Box 10, Lewisville, NC 27023
800.638.0928; 877.638.7576 (fax)
Visit us on the web at www.gryphonhouse.com.

Bulk Purchase
Gryphon House books are available for special premiums and sales promotions as well as for fund-raising use. Special editions or book excerpts also can be created to specifications. For details, call 800.638.0928.

Disclaimer
Gryphon House, Inc., cannot be held responsible for damage, mishap, or injury incurred during the use of or because of activities in this book. Appropriate and reasonable caution and adult supervision of children involved in activities and corresponding to the age and capability of each child involved are recommended at all times. When making choices about allowing children to participate in activities with certain ingredients, make sure to investigate possible toxicity and consider any food allergies or sensitivities. Do not leave children unattended at any time. Observe safety and caution at all times.

Library of Congress Cataloging-in-Publication Data
The Cataloging-in-Publication Data is registered with the Library of Congress for ISBN 978-0-87659-653-1.

Table of Contents

Introduction

Two-year-old Oliver sits quietly while his mother prepares his lunch. He is playing with one of his favorite toys, a miniature fire truck. Although the truck makes a siren noise and has flashing lights, Oliver prefers to hold the fire truck above his head as he alternates between spinning the wheels and rolling the truck back and forth along his face. Watching her son, Sara intervenes. "No, Oliver," Sara offers, "Like this." Taking a small police car and ambulance from a nearby bin, Sara begins rolling both toys on the kitchen floor. "See? Vroom, Vroom," Sara rubs Oliver's back to get his attention. Briefly, Oliver glances at Sara and then snatches both toys from her hands. Sara smiles at her son before she returns to making lunch. In possession of all three toys now, Oliver begins lining them end to end on the kitchen floor. As he finishes, Oliver looks at the toys, grinning as he stands on his toes and flaps his hands and arms. "Oliver," his mother says, "Time for lunch." Oliver continues to stare at the toys. "Oliver, lunchtime." There is still no response. "Oliver, it's time to stop." "Ollie?" "Ollie?" As Sara picks up her two-year-old to carry him to the table, her son's lack of response puzzles her. "Unbelievable," Sara says to herself, "It's almost like he doesn't even know his name."

In many families, the birth of a child is a joyous occasion. At first sight, parents have hopeful expectations for their babies, and as their children grow, so do these dreams. There are plans for birthday parties, school dances, college, successful careers, and grandchildren someday. The future seems endlessly promising.

Then something changes. The child seems different than other children his age. He doesn't babble. He rarely looks into his mother's eyes. He seems disinterested in other children. He never waves or points. Confusion, frustration, and panic begin to surface.

In sheer desperation, family members seek a professional evaluation. The results can be summed up in one simple sentence: "Your child has autism." From this point on, everything changes, and these four little words begin to alter the course of a family's life in dramatic ways.

Instead of playdates with peers, this child's most frequent social interaction comes from behavior specialists and outpatient therapists. Trips to the library, the park, and even the grocery store become a challenge for the family as problem behaviors become more and more frequent. Bystanders shake their heads with disapproval.

Family life is different now too. Brothers and sisters are hesitant around their sibling, unsure of what to say or how to act. Extended family and friends are equally cautious; many don't understand what it means to be "on the autism spectrum" and they are confused by the child's behaviors. Family get-togethers are now more of a burden than a celebration.

Finally, preschool begins. An early intervention classroom offers some relief. Here, there are other children with similar struggles and challenges. With support at home, the child makes tremendous progress. Two years pass quickly, and kindergarten awaits.

So many questions surround this new endeavor: What will school be like? How will my child behave in school? Will my child be able to learn? What will other children think of my child? Will the teacher be patient and supportive? Both family members and child are nervous and anxious on the first day of school, fearful of the unknown and unexpected.

As this situation illustrates, early childhood educators have tremendous responsibility for supporting these children and their families. It is a basic principle of human development that early experience affects later experience, and a child's first teachers are no exception to that precept. On these teachers' shoulders falls the weight of creating an accepting classroom environment that shapes and influences family and student attitudes toward school. The way in which early childhood teachers engage students with autism spectrum disorder (ASD) can have a significant and enduring impact on a child's success, not only academically, but also socially and emotionally.

All students can learn. Effective teachers expect all students to progress and they intervene with alternatives when best practices fail. These teachers recognize that every student has her own way of learning and they support daily success by identifying with the child and family, expanding their skill repertoire, and collaborating effectively with families, colleagues, and professionals from other fields.

This type of teacher attitude is especially important for students with ASD who often struggle to conform to traditional school expectations. For children with ASD, many common school behaviors, such as taking turns, sharing opinions, writing ideas, or simply sitting in a seat may pose significant challenges. Yet students with ASD can improve academic, social, and behavioral skills when teachers focus on individual strengths rather than deficits.

The purpose of this book is to showcase the capabilities of students with ASD and to prepare early childhood educators to work effectively with students with the multiple delays in basic functioning characteristic of pervasive developmental disorders like ASD. It guides teachers in understanding how ASD can affect student progress, and more important, how educators can tap into student potential. Each chapter includes several strategies that address specific academic, social, and behavioral needs common to many students with ASD. In addition, this book provides teachers with practical ways to help students with ASD feel like a part of their classroom community.

ASD affects every child differently. Often, the most effective classroom interventions use child-specific strengths and interests to engage students. This is why it is so important to get to know students with ASD and to build relationships with them and their families. These relationships help students feel more comfortable in the classroom and promote a sense of trust.

While this book is written specifically to offer strategies to help students with ASD achieve, many of the ideas suggested can help support general education students as well. These strategies can be integrated into class activities to offer all students alternative ways to build understanding. Furthermore, this book gives advice on how teachers can help all students learn to accept their classmates with ASD.

The number of students with ASD is growing quickly according to a 2015 report from the Centers for Disease Control and Prevention. Teachers have the power to effect change with this special population of students. Using strategies that allow students to access the curriculum in ways that build on their strengths promotes daily success in the classroom. ASD advocate and inclusion specialist Paula Kluth suggests that the way to create this type of inclusive classroom must begin with the teacher. In her book, *Don't We Already Do Inclusion?,* she notes that "the secret to creating change is to change." This is the focus of *Practical Strategies for Supporting Young Learners with Autism Spectrum Disorder.*

When early childhood educators encounter their first student on the autism spectrum, they are understandably concerned about their level of professional preparation, possible lack of experience, and doing the wrong thing. This book is designed to support teachers in this situation by building background, skills, and confidence. And because each child on the spectrum is unique, the book offers support to experienced educators, particularly those who are pushed to rethink their assumptions and teaching methods when a child's behavior sends them "back to the drawing board" in search of effective strategies.

Appreciating ASD: Beyond Misunderstandings and Misconceptions

It is one week before school begins and Ms. Sparks, a first-grade teacher, is excited to start another school year. As she looks over her class list, she recognizes one name almost immediately—Adam Washington. Ms. Sparks sighs heavily. Adam will be the first student with ASD that she will teach. Last year, Adam was in the kindergarten classroom across the hall from Ms. Sparks. Almost daily, Adam was carried off to the principal's office for disrupting the class. He rolled on the floor, threw books, and even hit his classmates. As a result of these behaviors, other children kept their distance. In fact, Ms. Sparks couldn't remember ever seeing Adam playing with other children at recess. And even though inclusion for students with ASD was the goal, Adam's previous teacher shared that this child often was excluded. Other students planned birthday parties, but Adam was not invited. On Valentine's Day, some children whose parents insisted that they give every classmate a card disposed of the card rather than deliver it to Adam. The work samples in Adam's school folder looked very different from those of the other students. He couldn't write his name, knew only four letters of the alphabet, and his drawings looked more like scribbling. Thinking about what she knows about Adam's time in kindergarten, Ms. Sparks suddenly feels overwhelmed with anxiety. She is frightened about her year ahead with Adam. She knows very little about ASD, and she is not sure how she will help Adam learn this school year. She begins searching for resources that will help her cope.

What Is ASD?

According to the Centers for Disease Control and Prevention, autism spectrum disorders are defined as "a group of developmental disabilities that can cause significant social, communication, and behavioral challenges." Although males are diagnosed with ASD four times as often as females, it can affect all races, ethnicities, and social classes. Currently, professionals cannot detect ASD through biological tests; and as a result, a diagnosis of ASD is based commonly on descriptions and observations of behaviors. This information is often collected from multiple sources, including parents, educators, and health professionals.

Some of the first descriptions of autism came from Leo Kanner and Hans Asperger. In 1943, Kanner observed a group of eleven children who had limited language and limited emotional interest in peers. During the same time, Asperger was observing four youths with similar social and behavioral issues. Both Kanner and Asperger used the term autistic to describe the observed developmental delays.

Despite this early discovery, autism was not recognized by the American Psychological Association (APA) until the 1980s. As the chief publication of the APA, the *Diagnostic and Statistical Manual of Mental Disorders, Fifth Edition (DSM-5)* is used to diagnose and categorize mental disorders. According to the *DSM-5*, individuals with ASD have deficits or delays in communication, social interaction, and behavior that can vary from mild to very severe. See table 1.1 listing examples of common ASD delays and deficits.

Previously, the autism heading included several separate diagnoses: autism, pervasive developmental disorder not otherwise specified (PDDNOS), Asperger syndrome (high-functioning autism), Rett syndrome, and childhood disintegrative disorder. Significant changes to the autism category occurred in 2013 when the *DSM-5* recognized all autism-related disorders as one general diagnosis. An additional change is the new symptom guidelines. These improved standards take into consideration the range of severity within the disorder, help professionals diagnose ASD more accurately, and suggest the level of support that is necessary for the child with ASD. See table 1.2 describing the differences in symptom severity.

Table 1.1 ASD Delays and Deficits

Communication	Social Interaction	Behavior
• No functional speech • Rigid or repetitive speech • Confusion with speech or conversational patterns	• Difficulty interpreting the emotions of others • Problems recognizing social cues • Difficulty making or keeping friends	• Restricted interests • Impulsivity • Repetitive play • Strong adherence to routine

Table 1.2 DSM-5 Levels of Severity for Autism Spectrum Disorders

Severity Level	Social Communication	Restrictive Behaviors
Level 3—Requires very significant support	Many language deficits that make social interaction difficult	Strong dependence on routines often influences daily activities
Level 2—Requires significant support	Some impairments in speaking and understanding, even with support	Routines define and frequently influence functioning in multiple settings
Level 1—Requires some support	Difficulty maintaining interest in others without some support	Routines hinder personal independence

Note: Adapted from American Psychiatric Association. 2013. *Diagnostic and Statistical Manual of Mental Disorders* (5th ed.). Washington, DC: American Psychiatric Association.

Determining Delays

Being able to identify delays in children with ASD helps teachers address individual students' needs. Read the following classroom scenarios. Determine whether each describes a communication, social, or behavior concern. After you are finished, check your answers below.

1. Ray loves monkeys. In writing class, Ray writes about monkeys almost every day.

2. At home, Karen has a favorite cartoon show and will have a tantrum if the channel is changed or she is interrupted while watching it. When Karen's teacher greets her, Karen responds with dialogue from the television show.

3. Troy drops his lunch on the floor. George laughs when the orange rolls under the table.

4. During free play, Hayden stacks blocks in a tower over and over again. He pushes classmates away when they ask to play with him.

5. Jessie's teacher tells her to take a little cat nap at recess time. Jessie starts racing around the room and, when asked why she is doing this, she makes a meowing sound. She is literally looking for a cat.

6. The children are in the dress-up corner trying on different clothing. When a girl places a hat on Hakim and hugs him, he becomes very agitated, throws the hat on the floor, and begins flapping his hands.

7. On the first day of kindergarten, some of the children cry when their parents leave. Melissa crawls underneath the teacher's desk and refuses to come out. If anyone approaches her, she screams.

Answers
1. behavior; 2. communication; 3. social; 4. social; 5. communication; 6. behavior; and 7. behavior/communication.

Why Is Autism a Spectrum Disorder?

It is often said that "if you know one child with ASD, you know one child with ASD." The meaning behind this phrase is that no two children with ASD are alike. Every child with ASD will have his own set of symptoms, strengths, and weaknesses. Each of these elements will affect how a child with ASD behaves, thinks, and feels.

The diversity among individuals with the disorder is why autism is considered a spectrum disorder. The abilities of students with ASD are on a continuum and they influence how well a child functions in school and community settings. It is important for early childhood educators to have the knowledge and skills to help students with ASD progress in school.

ASD Fast Facts for Teachers

Test your knowledge of ASD. Do you agree or disagree with the following statements?

Circle the response that indicates your level of agreement with each statement.

Strongly Agree (SA), Agree (A), Undecided (U) Disagree (D) or Strongly Disagree (SD)

1. In the United States, about 1 in 100 individuals has ASD.

    SA   A   U   D   SD

2. The number of students with ASD in federally-funded schools is insignificant.

    SA   A   U   D   SD

3. The vast majority of students with ASD spend at least some portion of the school day in the general education classroom.

    SA   A   U   D   SD

4. Greater awareness of ASD has led to more reliable diagnoses.

    SA   A   U   D   SD

5. If a student has ASD, he cannot be diagnosed with another disorder.

    SA   A   U   D   SD

6. More boys than girls are affected by ASD.

    SA   A   U   D   SD

7. A diagnosis of ASD indicates that the child cannot be expected to make significant progress.

    SA   A   U   D   SD

8. ASD is the fastest growing developmental disorder.

    SA   A   U   D   SD

9. Treatment of ASD cannot begin until the child begins formal schooling.

    SA   A   U   D   SD

10. Once a child with ASD is diagnosed in a family, every other child will have some form of the disorder.

    SA   A   U   D   SD

Responses

1. *Disagree*. The Centers for Disease Control and Prevention reports that about one in sixty-eight individuals has the disorder in the United States.

2. *Disagree*. According to the U.S. Department of Education National Center for Education Statistics (2013), more than 300,000 students with ASD are enrolled in federally funded school programs.

3. *Agree*. Under the mandates of the Individuals with Disabilities Education Act (IDEA), the majority of students with ASD spend some part of the school day with their typically developing peers.

4. *Agree*. Not only are professionals able to identify specific ASD traits, but also significant differences in how those traits present in individual children. For instance, communication delays may appear in one child as scripted speech and in another child as very limited functional speech.

5. *Disagree*. An individual with ASD can also be diagnosed with additional disorders. For example, a child with ASD might also have a diagnosis of Down syndrome.

6. *Agree*. ASD affects all races, ethnicities, and social classes, but males are diagnosed four times as often as females.

7. *Disagree*. A diagnosis of ASD will affect how students learn, but it does not make it impossible for students to make academic and social progress. With appropriate interventions, many individuals with ASD lead happy, productive lives.

8. *Agree*. Over the last twenty years, the prevalence rate of ASD has risen steadily. Nonetheless, ASD research is poorly funded.

9. *Disagree*. Under the Early Intervention Program for Infants and Toddlers with Disabilities, Part C of IDEA, children with ASD qualify for free, federally funded services that provide access to speech and language therapy and behavioral therapy for children with developmental disorders and their families.

10. *Disagree*. Siblings of children with ASD are not guaranteed to have the disorder. However, families with children already diagnosed with ASD are at greater risk of having additional children with ASD than the general population.

ASD Early Warning Signs

As a teacher of a student with ASD, you may wonder how a student with ASD receives her diagnosis. For many young children, it begins with a caregiver noticing some specific early warning signs. Although all children will follow their own development paths, caregivers and educators should view persistent social, behavioral, and communication deficits cautiously. When children are diagnosed with ASD at an earlier age, they often have a better chance of developing useful skills. Further, early detection can lead to more effective and relevant treatment plans.

Many children with ASD will show signs of impaired social and communication development before age three. However, students with more functional skills are sometimes diagnosed later. This is why it is important for teachers to be aware of early warning signs too. Although a child who has one or two of the following behaviors may not necessarily receive an ASD diagnosis, a child with several of the following early signs of ASD might need further evaluation:

- lack of eye contact
- repetitive or isolated play
- difficulty engaging in imaginative play
- intensive dependence on routine
- limited understanding of others' feelings
- echo speech (imitating words that were just spoken)
- difficulty maintaining conversation
- repetitive behaviors
- self-injurious behaviors (for example, hitting or biting oneself)
- dislike of physical touch
- frequent tantrums
- difficulty distinguishing familiar people from strangers

Diagnosing ASD

Diagnosing a child with ASD can be a long and complex process. Often, it is parents or care-givers who first notice differences in their child's development. Parents might be prompted to have an evaluation by a pediatrician if their child does not talk or show interest in others by age two. In fact, this is the age that most families seek help and diagnosis. If further evaluation is deemed necessary, a child will be seen by a psychiatrist, who uses a collection of evidence including input from parents, doctors, teachers, and caregivers, as well as her own observations to make a diagnosis.

Greater awareness of ASD and its characteristics have improved the diagnosis process tremendously. It is now possible to reliably diagnose a child with ASD by age two. However, it is possible for students with high-functioning capabilities to receive an ASD

diagnosis later in childhood or even as a young adult. Also, given that the underlying causes of autism and an understanding of the spectrum is just emerging, it is possible for an individual who is high functioning and was not diagnosed as a child to come to this realization as an older adult.

As an educator, it can be tempting to label a child in the classroom as "autistic" based on observed behaviors. However, it is important to remember that diagnosing a child with ASD is based on many factors, not simply one teacher's perspective. It is a basic principle of assessment that important decisions—such as a diagnosis of autism spectrum disorders—should not be based solely on one source of information. It takes multiple perspectives collected over a period of time to arrive at any meaningful diagnosis.

If a child is suspected of having ASD, following these steps can help secure support for the child:

- Document observed behaviors in the classroom. Begin a file of the child's specific actions and, whenever possible, the events that prompted the behaviors.
- Communicate regularly with parents. Be sure that parents know your concerns and solicit insight to solve problems within the classroom.
- Discuss your concerns about the student with school or center administrators. Provide weekly or monthly updates about behavior and academic progress.
- Collaborate with the special education professionals in the school. Implement strategies that can support the student within the general education classroom.
- Increase your understanding and awareness of ASD. Review current journals on inclusive practices for students with ASD.

Common Misconceptions about ASD

Autism has gained a great deal of attention recently. What was once a mysterious and rare diagnosis has become far more commonplace. However, myths about the disorder are still widespread. Misinformation about ASD can limit student potential and achievement. This is why educators, especially, must be aware of accurate information about ASD. The following are some of the most common misconceptions about ASD.

- **Myth: ASD is caused by uncaring parents.** In the early years of autism study, parenting styles were often blamed as the cause of the disorder. In particular, mothers with an obsession for perfection or a strict demeanor were thought to be more likely to have a child with autism. These maternal influences were believed to cause children to be more socially isolated. Autism is now widely accepted as a neurodevelopmental disorder. Moreover, many educators today acknowledge the substantial role that parents can play in supporting a child with autism in the school environment.

  Just imagine the damage that was done in the past when parents were blamed for causing the disorder in their children. It surely had a negative effect on family relationships and prevented children on the autism spectrum from achieving their full potential. Although professionals no longer attribute the disorder to poor parenting, this does not mean that parents no longer feel responsible in some way. Parents may feel guilty that they did not recognize the symptoms earlier and seek professional help sooner. They may continue to encounter people—even uninformed or misinformed members of their families—who persist in thinking a type A mother is responsible for the child's condition.

- **Myth: Vaccines are the cause of ASD.** Currently, scientists cannot identify the cause of ASD. However, studies have not shown that vaccines cause ASD. Instead, research points to genetics as a major influence. As Cynthia Saulnier and Pamela Venntola find, this perspective explains why families with one child with ASD are more likely to have another child with the disorder. Awareness about this genetic link to ASD can also cause great distress for a family member who feels that the "bad genes" he or she contributed are the culprit. Worries about this genetic connection might cause a parent to cope by denying signs of the disorder, and this lack of acknowledgment could delay accurate diagnosis and treatment.

- **Myth: Autism can be cured.** Many parents still believe that if only they could afford an expensive private-school program, then their child could be cured. Although many interventions have been proven successful for students with ASD, no strategy will cure a child of ASD. It is a chronic developmental disorder, and individuals with ASD will always have the disorder. However, with caring and supportive parents and professionals, many youths with ASD can learn to manage behaviors and lead productive, happy lives.

- **Myth: Autism is a disease.** Autism is classified as a biological disorder that affects brain development. Studies by Nancy Minshew and Timothy Keller show that brain imaging of children with ASD has identified differences in brain development distinct to youths with the disorder. Individuals with ASD are born with the disorder; it is not contagious in any way.

- **Myth: Students with ASD are generally aggressive.** Although the media may be quick to highlight individual cases of violent ASD behaviors, students with ASD typically do not lash out at others with the intent to inflict injury. It is far more common for students with ASD to be withdrawn than to be physically violent with their peers. When students with ASD do exhibit challenging behaviors, it is usually in response to frustration with their inability to communicate their wants and needs. This is one reason why it is so important to help children on the autism spectrum to reach their full potential in language. Verbal and linguistic intelligence supports not only academic growth but also social interaction.

- **Myth: Students with ASD cannot build social relationships.** Certainly, social relationships are more difficult for students with ASD to build and maintain. However, students with ASD, like typically developing students, can learn to share interests with others. These relationships can help children with ASD increase their confidence, show empathy for others, and learn functional skills. Early childhood educators' use of interventions that support students with ASD in having positive interactions with their classmates can ensure that the child is included.

- **Myth: All students with ASD behave and learn similarly.** ASD is such a complex disorder because it can present so differently in individuals. Some children on the autism spectrum have multiple disabilities and others may be intellectually gifted. This is one of the reasons ASD is a spectrum disorder. Students with ASD vary in having minor delays in communication and social functioning to profound developmental delays. For instance, one child diagnosed with the disorder might be virtually nonverbal, another might repeat words and phrases, and yet another might be quite talkative and capable of conversation— particularly on a topic of intense interest. Further, strengths in one area do not

guarantee strengths across symptoms. This explains why a child with advanced vocabulary could have very poor social skills.

- **Myth: Most children with ASD have exceptional talents.** Most people are familiar with the movie *Rain Man* and may assume that a child on the autism spectrum is brilliant in one domain. For example, popular media portray individuals with amazing skills in mathematics, the arts, technology, or with a so-called *photographic* (eidetic) memory. A person with this pattern of behavior is referred to as an *autistic savant*. It means that there is at least one type of intelligence in which the person is a genius and has abilities that are far outside the capabilities of the great majority of other people. In real life, autistic savants are quite rare and make up only about 10 percent of the ASD population, as Darold Treffert noted in a 2009 journal article.

- **Myth: There are universal interventions for students with ASD.** When working with children who have pervasive developmental disorders, a one-size approach definitely does not fit all. With so much variance among students with ASD, universally effective interventions are simply impossible. In addition, the instructional practices for students with ASD change frequently. In many cases, educators have to create customized supports to address the specific needs and challenges of individual students with ASD.

- **Myth: Children with ASD perform best in specialized special education classrooms.** Similar to any other intervention, the educational setting must be matched with the strengths and needs of an individual student. Certainly, some children achieve more in classrooms specially designed to meet the needs of children with ASD. However, many students with ASD can and do benefit from inclusion. Interacting with typically developing peers can help students with ASD practice social and communication skills in a natural setting.

Types of Special Education Placements

The Individuals with Disabilities Education Act (IDEA) mandates that students with disabilities be placed in the "least restrictive environment." This means that students with disabilities, including students with ASD, should have as many opportunities as possible to learn alongside their typically developing peers. In addition, IDEA protects students with disabilities from being removed from general education classrooms unless their goals cannot be met with reasonable supports and services.

In order to receive federal funding, public schools must follow all mandates of IDEA. While school officials may certainly go beyond the requirements of IDEA, the minimum standards set by the law are required. In order to meet a wide array of students' needs, the law requires a continuum of services. Children with ASD will most likely receive service through one of the placements described in table 1.3.

Regardless of educational placement, appropriate learning goals are important. Such goals are often included within an individualized family service plan (IFSP) or an individualized education program (IEP). Children with disabilities who are younger than three years old have early intervention services outlined by an IFSP. The local school district organizes and implements the IEP for preschool and school-age children. Both the IFSP and IEP outline the educational and developmental goals for children with disabilities. Both plans also name who will deliver services, how progress will be monitored and assessed, and what classroom accommodations will be provided.

Maintaining a Positive Attitude

Educating a child with ASD can be both rewarding and challenging. Students with ASD, like their typically developing peers, need to feel accepted and valued in their classroom. Teachers should make every effort to help students with ASD feel productive, be warmly welcomed into the classroom, and contribute to the school community. In order to do so, teachers must maintain a positive attitude about including students with ASD.

Set high expectations for learners with ASD. Students cannot be measured by their disabilities. Early childhood educators should have high expectations for students with ASD. It is important to communicate those expectations to the student and his support team. Students with ASD develop skills over time just as other students do. Just because a child with ASD begins the school year not reading does not mean she will never read.

Get to know each student with ASD as an individual. Each student with ASD is unique. Do not assume that each child with ASD you teach will have the same needs or will respond

Table 1.3 Common Special Education Placements for Students with ASD

Placement	Description of Services
Itinerant services	The student spends much of the school day in a general education classroom with support from specially designed instruction or services based on individual needs.
Self-contained special education classrooms	Within a general education school environment, the student receives instruction in a special education classroom on either a full-time or part-time basis. Often, students are assigned to these classrooms based on needs or skill level.
Specialized private-school setting	The student is taught in a private-school setting that has a specialized focus on students with major developmental delays, a disability, or multiple delays or disorders.

to the same interventions. Instead, take the time to learn the strengths and needs of individual students.

Celebrate milestones. Students with ASD may be delayed in reaching developmental milestones (such as writing their names, tying their shoes, and buttoning their coats). No matter when a child with ASD accomplishes a goal, celebrate the accomplishment. Teach other students to be sensitive to differences in developmental growth as well.

Recognize and appreciate the diversity ASD offers. Teaching a student with ASD has many benefits. It helps educators learn to be more flexible and creative in their instruction while expanding their understanding of child development. Building an appreciation for diversity among learners allows educators to be more open to novel approaches toward teaching and learning.

How ASD Affects Classroom Behaviors and Learning

Many factors affect how students with ASD interact with their environments. Sights, smells, and noises can distract some children with ASD from learning activities. Changes to routines can be highly disruptive, making it a struggle for students to stay focused. Similarly, delays in speech make it more difficult for young children with ASD to express their feelings. For instance, if a child is expecting to have recess after lunch but cannot play because of rain, then he may feel upset and begin screaming or crying. This child with ASD reacts to change with challenging behaviors because he lacks the words to communicate his needs. These behaviors can limit the progress of students with ASD and typically developing learners alike when they are not addressed.

Think back to the teacher described at the beginning of this chapter; she has much to learn about ASD. As a starting point, she will have to learn to appreciate the strengths and needs of individual students on the autism spectrum and be hopeful about their potential. She will need to locate authoritative sources of information, research-based support, and the resources in her community. As she learns more about Adam, she will be able to address behavioral concerns and support his academic growth. Throughout the school year, the teacher will need to guide Adam and his classmates in positive social interaction. In addition, the teacher will need to work effectively with Adam's family, her colleagues, and professionals in other fields to achieve the best possible outcomes for this child.

This book will provide practical strategies to address these social, academic, and behavioral challenges of early childhood students with ASD. The remaining eight chapters will discuss how students with ASD process information and their environments. Additionally, each chapter will suggest appropriate interventions that can engage and support these young learners. Strategies will be outlined, explained in steps, and, where appropriate, linked to grade-appropriate IEP goals. Each chapter will also include a list of technology resources that teachers can use to plan and support instruction.

While the strategies offered in this book are based on the best practices for teaching students with ASD, educators should remember that each child with ASD is unique. Students with ASD achieve most when interventions are appropriately matched with students' interests and skills and when instruction is planned to meet individual needs. To begin this process, teachers must first establish an inclusive classroom community.

Technology Resources to Support ASD Awareness in Educators

- Autism Speaks (https://www.autismspeaks.org/) is one of the most authoritative websites on ASD awareness. Specific news, blogs, resources, and tool kits are available for individual age groups.

- General background information is available at Organization for Autism Research (http://www.researchautism.org/family/index.asp). The website text is available in eleven different languages. Information on ASD research, home and school interventions, and family supports is provided.

- The U.S. Department of Health and Human Services (http://www.hhs.gov/autism/) is a good place to start when researching general autism awareness. Find information on the diagnosis and treatment processes here.

- Join an ASD research community at Interactive Autism Network (http://www.iancommunity.org/cs/about_asds/pddnos). Use this website as a library of the latest findings on autism spectrum disorders.

- The Autism Society (http://www.autism-society.org/) has several resources just for education professionals. Review the online database for services and supports for individuals with ASD throughout the nation.

- Use the Thinking Person's Guide to Autism (www.thinkingautismguide.com/p/mission-statement.html) to see ASD through the eyes of actual individuals with the disorder. Read essays that parents, professionals, and friends have written to share their experiences and knowledge of ASD.

- Get information at Research Autism (http://www.researchautism.net/) to guide and support your own professional development. Review current interventions and publications on this website.

- Read about some of the effective strategies for working with students with ASD at the Association for Science in Autism Treatment (http://www.asatonline.org/). Click on the tab for Parents & Educators to learn more about treatment plans and how to advocate for students with ASD.

- Visit the Autism Research Institute (http://www.autism.com/) to read daily facts about ASD and individual achievements of people with the disorder. Also, stay current with ASD research and increasing diagnoses.

- Temple Grandin (http://templegrandin.com) talks about her experiences growing up with ASD. Questions about the disorder can be submitted to her for discussion and response.

Key Terms

autism or autism spectrum disorder (ASD): A disability that is characterized by developmental delays in communication, social interaction, and behavior. Autism is called a spectrum disorder because individuals with the disability vary greatly based on a continuum of symptoms or traits.

general education: Sometimes referred to as regular education; refers to the curriculum designed to help all students reach state standards that are measured annually through state assessments required formerly by the No Child Left Behind Act and in coming years guided by the Every Student Succeeds Act.

the Individuals with Disabilities Education Act (IDEA): The law that requires schools to provide educational services to students with disabilities.

individualized education program (IEP): Plans the educational goals, supports, and services for school-age children.

individualized family service plan (IFSP): Organizes the early intervention goals for children from birth to age three.

itinerant services: Supports that assist students with disabilities while they are in the general education environment.

least-restrictive environment (LRE): Requires that students with disabilities be included with nondisabled peers to the greatest extent possible.

savant: An individual with exceptional abilities in a specific area of study, such as mathematics or art.

typically developing peer or classmate: Students without identified disabilities.

2 ASD in the Classroom: Effective Inclusion

It is the first day of school in Ms. Rosen's classroom. For the past week, Ms. Rosen has been preparing her classroom to welcome twenty-two first graders. As she waits for the start of the day, Ms. Rosen looks around the classroom. All four classroom walls are covered with colorful decorations. Every window has transparent clings posted on it. The bulletin boards are covered with brightly colored paper and class alphabet posters outlined in glitter trims and sparkling borders. Although the classroom is stocked with furniture, Ms. Rosen has purchased additional pieces to fill large, open spaces around the room. To direct students through the maze of desks and tables, Ms. Rosen has painted child-sized footprints on the tiled floors. Hanging from above are laminated figures of the class mascot, Rosen's Reading Rabbits. The cardboard rabbits hang only inches above the teacher's head, making a soft screeching sound as the clips they hang from slide back and forth along the light fixtures. Each desk has a large nameplate pasted on top of it. There are also chair sacks hanging from each student chair. The desks are arranged into clusters to facilitate group work. The only exception is one desk, which is positioned directly next to the teacher's desk. This seat is for Kate, a student with ASD. Ms. Rosen chose this special place for Kate to limit distractions for both her and the other students. Ms. Rosen takes one final look to make sure that everything in the classroom is in place. Just before the children file into the school, she lightly sprays the classroom with a flowery air freshener. As students begin to arrive, Ms. Rosen sees Kate coming down the hallway with her mother. Sensing that Kate might be nervous about starting school, Ms. Rosen crouches down close to Kate's face and says, "Come see your new classroom!" In response, Kate runs away to hide in the coat cubbies. "Now what?" Ms. Rosen thinks to herself, "How am I supposed to have an inclusive classroom?"

The Value of Inclusion

Special education law guarantees all students, regardless of ability, equal opportunities to learn. Inclusion is one way to provide students with disabilities a quality education. When students with disabilities are assigned to inclusive classrooms, they can improve their social acceptance, academic progress, and self-confidence. Furthermore, inclusion helps students with disabilities to become functioning, productive members of society.

However, there are many aspects to consider when planning inclusion for students with ASD. General awareness of the disability is absolutely necessary to plan the classroom environment effectively. It is also important to understand individual characteristics of students with ASD. Take, for instance, the opening vignette from this chapter: Ms. Rosen has invested time, energy, and even her own money in making her classroom look attractive. In fact, many of her students will probably be mesmerized by the colorful and eye-catching displays; but Kate is over-stimulated by the sights, sounds, and smells of the classroom. Meeting with Kate and her family before the first day of school to discuss the child's behavioral responses may have prevented Kate's adverse reaction to the classroom.

In addition, Ms. Rosen's view of inclusion needs to be challenged. Her decision to separate Kate from her peers in the class implies that she expects Kate to be a behavior problem and that she has lower expectations for students with ASD. There is no way for the teacher to know how Kate will respond in a group of her peers without giving her a chance to interact. By isolating Kate before ever meeting her, Ms. Rosen's actions contradict her words about inclusion; she may be "talking the talk" but definitely is not "walking the walk," as the old saying goes. Consequently, Kate and her classmates are missing out on the opportunity to grow socially.

When teachers are prepared to support students with ASD, inclusion can improve the entire learning environment. Inclusion that is not planned thoughtfully, however, can be stressful and frustrating for teachers and students. This is why teachers must be aware of the challenges to inclusion and must implement strategies to address these needs.

Challenges to Including Students with ASD

Even when educators plan for successful inclusion of students with ASD, there will still be challenges. The academic ability of students with ASD varies greatly, especially in the primary grades. While some children with ASD experience learning delays, many others perform at or above grade level. In addition—just like their typically developing peers—academic struggles can vary among and within different subject areas. For instance, in language arts a child could excel at decoding the words in a printed text but have difficulty with comprehension questions, particularly those that focus on a character's intentions and motives. Meanwhile, another child with ASD could outperform most peers in mathematics but struggle with writing—both handwriting and story writing. In either case, teachers must recognize the differences among their students with ASD and plan instruction to meet their individual learning needs.

Including students with ASD can produce social concerns as well. Certainly, one of the most prominent characteristics of ASD is social deficits. Social awkwardness coupled with communication delays make it more difficult for students with ASD to initiate and maintain friendships. Additionally, because of their young age, typically developing peers may struggle to understand why their classmates with ASD behave so differently. If teachers fail to recognize their need for social supports, students with ASD can feel isolated in a general education classroom, even one that claims to be inclusive.

Some of the greatest inclusion challenges, however, focus on managing students' behaviors. Although some students with ASD have few behavioral concerns, others will have many developmental delays that can inhibit progress. The severity of behaviors will also vary. As Johnny Matson and Marie Nebel-Schwalm point out in their journal article about challenging behaviors, the most common problem behaviors of ASD will fall into one of four categories:

- Perseverative behaviors
- Aggressive (challenging) behavior
- Self-injurious behavior
- Noncompliance

Perseverative Behaviors

As Roberto Militerni and his colleagues outlined in their journal article about repetitive behaviors, *perseveration* is repetitive behavior that may or may not have practical reasoning for the action. Perseverative behaviors are also referred to as *stereotypical behaviors, self-stimulatory behaviors,* or *stimming,* because children may be attempting to increase or reduce their sensory stimulation. Common perseverations in young children include the following:

- Hand flapping
- Rocking
- Face rubbing (ears, nose, mouth, and so on)
- Pacing
- Chinning (rubbing chin on parts of the body, such as arms or hands)
- Scripting (repeating words or phrases)

- Perseverative thoughts (internalized thinking or scripting about a single idea or concept, such as computers or trains)

Occupational therapy research by Eynat Gal and her colleagues suggests that perseveration may help individuals with ASD cope with different levels of sensory stimulation. A noisy, busy classroom can easily overwhelm a student with ASD. Seemingly minor distractions in the classroom—a squeaky door or ticking clock—can pose powerful anxiety for some children with ASD. Alternatively, a classroom without constant stimulation can be equally distressing for other children with the disorder. These environmental stressors from either too much or too little stimulation along with classroom demands may lead to challenging behaviors. Engaging in perseverative thoughts or activities is one way some children with ASD deal with these feelings of agitation.

Aggressive (Challenging) Behavior

Aggressive behavior is defined as actions that are intended to inflict harm on someone else. Given that young children on the autism spectrum rarely intend to hurt others, their socially unacceptable behavior would be better described as a challenging behavior. Challenging behaviors refer to those actions that are socially unacceptable and include pushing, hitting, grabbing, scratching, spitting, kicking, and destroying property. Although these behaviors can be distressing, it is important to remember that they are rarely personally directed. A number of factors can prompt challenging behaviors. Changes to routines can be confusing or frustrating to students with ASD and can lead to disruptive behaviors. Some children with ASD may express wants or needs through impulsive behaviors. For instance, a child might push a peer to get to a favorite book or grab the arm of an adult who is blocking the water fountain. Similarly, when students with ASD are unable to use functional speech to communicate, they may rely on actions to show their emotions. Ripping classwork could communicate "I am tired" or "This work is too difficult."

Self-Injurious Behavior

Some children with ASD engage in self-injurious behaviors. These behaviors purposefully inflict harm, and if not managed, can cause long-term physical damage. Head banging, hitting parts of the body, pinching, biting, and picking at scabs or sores are common self-injurious behaviors. According to Shirley Cohen in her book *Targeting Autism,* the motivation for self-injurious behaviors is unclear and may possibly vary by individual. Some theories suggest that these behaviors are a way to escape other pain or injury, such as headaches or overstimulation. Other research points to self-stimulation as the root cause. Some research has also identified chronic medical disorders, such as chemical imbalances and seizure disorders, as causes for these behaviors.

Noncompliance

When a child does not follow directions, he is noncompliant. Delays or deficits in communication skills often prompt noncompliance in children with ASD. When students are unable to express their wants or needs or simply do not understand what is expected of them, they will not complete a task. Additionally, students may be noncompliant as a way to communicate anxiety or frustration. Unexpected changes to routines or schedules can produce feelings of insecurity that trigger noncompliance in young children who don't have the skills to articulate their feelings. On its own, noncompliance can be very challenging but it is especially demanding when it escalates to more severe behaviors. Tantrums, bolting (leaving an assigned area without permission), or aggressive behaviors can develop easily from noncompliance. As a result, it is

important that teachers recognize and address noncompliant behavior in the classroom.

Sensory Sensitivity

Students with ASD may be under- or oversensitive to their environments. Children with sensory hypersensitivity feel stress or anxiety from common sight, sound, or tactile experiences. For instance, a child with ASD may be bothered by the buzzing of fluorescent lights or the feel of a clothing label against his skin. Conversely, children who are sensory hyposensitive feel stress or anxiety when their bodies do not receive enough sensory input. Students with sensory hyposensitivity use the environment around them to create additional stimulation. For example, a child with sensory hyposensitivity might slide his feet repeatedly on the carpet at story time or apply excessive pressure while coloring or writing.

There are several ways to address problem behaviors in students with ASD. Teachers must assess challenging behaviors quickly and carefully to provide the most effective support with the least disruptions to the class environment. Planning this type of teacher response takes practice. Looking at table 2.1 consider the classroom examples of common ASD problem behaviors listed in column 2. Use these guiding questions to determine how these behaviors might be addressed in school:

- How might you respond to each of the behaviors described in the Classroom Example column?
- How are these behaviors disrupting learning for the student or his peers?
- What safety concerns are present for students with ASD and the other students?
- Is it possible to prevent some of these behaviors?

Then, compare your answers with the possible responses described in column 3.

Table 2.1 Classroom Examples of Common ASD Problem Behaviors and Possible Responses

Problem Behavior	Classroom Example	Possible Responses
Perseverative Behaviors	Student refuses to start his math work until he has placed all of the classroom computers in standby mode.	Assign the child a "student helper" position. Allow the child to close down and store the computers before class begins.
	A three-year-old interacts with others by pretending to grasp something in the air and then offering it to the other person.	Use the student's behavior to spur conversation. Encourage the child to use words or phrases to label what he is offering to others.
Aggressive or Challenging Behaviors	Student hits the teacher when she tells the class recess is over.	Give the student warnings prior to the end of recess. Use a timer or warning signal to let the student know when he has ten, five, and two minutes until the close of recess.
	After the winners of an art contest have their work posted on a bulletin board in the hallway, a student rips them off the board and tears them into pieces.	Help the child repair the torn artwork. Model appropriate ways to congratulate the contest winners.
Self-Injurious Behaviors	Student picks at scabs during story time until she is bleeding.	Use strategies to keep the student engaged during the story. Ask questions about the story or encourage the child to draw pictures of her favorite part on a lapboard.
	When a child does not get a turn to hold the classroom rabbit, he begins to hit his forehead on the floor.	Create a visual schedule using pictures that show when the child will get to hold the rabbit. Reference the schedule frequently while the child waits.
Noncompliant Behaviors	Student will not come to the carpet for story time when outdoor play is canceled due to frigid temperatures and ice.	Replace recess with another preferred activity. Place a picture of this activity on the schedule. Show the child when this activity will occur on the schedule.
	A three-year-old refuses to use fingerpaint and hides in the reading corner.	Use a visual chart (see *First, Then* Boards in Chapter 6) to help the child understand that once the nonpreferred activity is complete, a preferred activity can be earned.
Sensory Sensitivity	Student will not complete her reading work because the fluorescent lights are "noisy." She begins to cry loudly.	Provide the student with headphones to limit the lighting noise.
	When the fire alarm sounds, a child begins to run around in circles and hyperventilate.	Whenever possible, determine when the fire alarm will sound. Prepare the child for the sound by describing its volume, noise, and duration. Provide the child with earmuffs or headphones to muffle the sound.

Benefits to Including Students with ASD

Often, inclusion is viewed as valuable only to students with disabilities. However, effective inclusion programs have advantages for the entire school community. Educating students with ASD in general education classrooms can impact instructional practices, student self-confidence, and class unity. The degree of this type of influence is highly dependent on the attitude the teacher has toward the inclusion process. Educators must be willing to recognize the potential of inclusion and to work with colleagues and students to support different types of learners.

Collaboration

No one expects a general education teacher to have extensive knowledge of the best practices of teaching students with ASD. This is why teacher collaboration is both a necessity and a benefit of inclusion practices. When special and general education teachers work together, they are better able to address the specific needs of students with ASD in an inclusive setting. Teacher collaboration allows educators to contribute their unique expertise to solve academic, behavioral, or social student concerns. Although the initial focus of collaboration may be only on students with ASD, collaboration helps to develop teacher knowledge and skills that enhance the learning of all students. This is especially true in early childhood classrooms where abstract topics can be challenging for the majority of students.

Collaboration among school staff members works best when teachers coordinate the strengths and needs of the student with teachers' knowledge. This process can take some planning to be effective. See figure 2.1 showing the Collaborative Support Map, which educators can use to develop a collaboration team for individual students with ASD. This organizer outlines not only who will collaborate, but also how teachers can contribute to students' learning.

Figure 2.1 Collaboration Support Map

Within the circle segments of this graphic organizer, list teachers and staff who could contribute to a collaboration team for a student with ASD in your classroom. In the gray rectangular boxes, include the type of support they could offer either to your instructional planning or the student's inclusion plan.

Example:

Name and role—Mrs. Joanna Smith, director of Happy Time Preschool

Type of support—Provide feedback on lesson plans; suggest adaptations for class activities; participate in meetings with the family

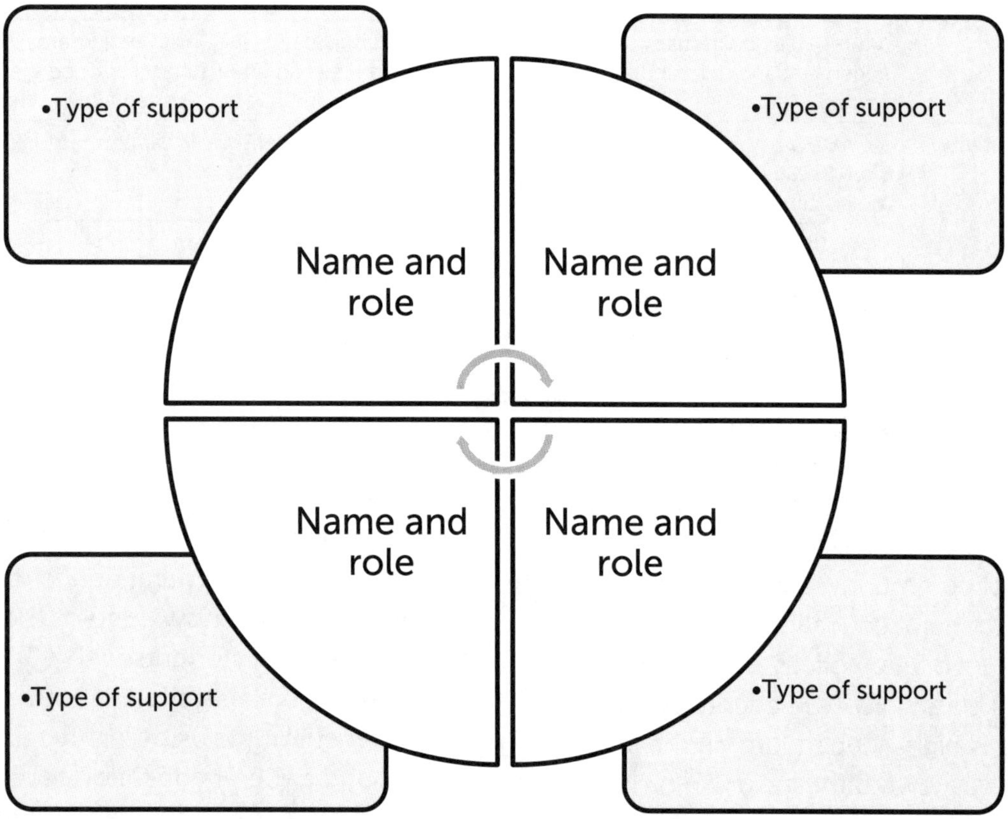

- Type of support
- Type of support

Name and role

Name and role

Name and role

Name and role

- Type of support
- Type of support

Social Skills Building

Another benefit of the inclusion of students with ASD is social skills building. Students with social delays learn skills through observation and interaction.

Although team-building activities may not inspire genuine friendships, this type of interaction can develop social growth for students with ASD, who are often withdrawn. Looking to their peers as models, students with ASD can learn to participate more fully in classroom and social activities. Typically developing peers, conversely, will learn to work with others who have different learning styles and skill sets. In the process, both students grow in self-confidence, which can directly affect their classroom progress and achievement.

Awareness of ASD

Perhaps the greatest benefit of ASD inclusion is increased awareness of the disorder. Young children, especially, are curious or cautious of peers who are different from them. Cooperative learning allows typically developing students to learn more about their peers with ASD. This type of interaction allows other students to get to know more about ASD, making children with the disorder more approachable.

Similarly, inclusion of students with ASD challenges teachers to look beyond a limited understanding of the diagnosis. Educating several different students with ASD broadens teachers' awareness of ASD and helps them create a repertoire of effective interventions. Inclusion also encourages teachers to view students with ASD as individuals and to set learning expectations that are based on specific strengths and needs. However, this outcome is only possible if educators are prepared to teach in inclusive classrooms.

Preparing to Teach Students with ASD

Teaching students with ASD in inclusive classrooms is demanding. To implement appropriate supports and strategies, teachers must have knowledge and understanding of ASD. When teachers are aware of how ASD affects the learning process, they are better prepared to plan effective interventions. Such adjustments to the learning environment and curriculum are important to student progress.

Educators must plan thoughtfully to teach students with ASD. Although a universal ASD-focused curriculum is not yet available, researchers agree that many students with ASD can benefit from a structured classroom setting with age-appropriate practices. So while planning the content of class lessons is important, teachers must also give careful attention to the learning environment, rules, and expectations for all students and class routines.

Arranging the Classroom Environment

Many primary teachers use colorful decorations to make their classrooms feel warm and inviting. However, even general fixtures in the classroom, such as lights, windows, and doors, can provide too much sensory input for students with ASD. With the addition of an abundance of displays and embellishments, classrooms can be overstimulating and distracting to students with ASD.

As a result, inclusive classrooms should be organized in a way that allows students to feel comfortable and safe. For students with ASD, this means classrooms are neat, orderly, and generally calming. It is also important to learn the sensory triggers of individual students and avoid these stimuli to the greatest extent possible. Use the checklist that follows to self-assess your preparedness to organize an inclusive classroom for students with ASD. If you respond "no" to a statement, plan appropriate adjustments to your current practices.

Checklist for Organizing an Inclusive Classroom for Students with ASD

I keep the classroom neat and organized.

❏ Yes ❏ No

I teach my students to keep their personal space organized.

❏ Yes ❏ No

My classroom is clutter free.

❏ Yes ❏ No

I inventory supplies regularly and purge unnecessary items.

❏ Yes ❏ No

When seating children in groups, I include all students.

❏ Yes ❏ No

I believe that every child, including students with ASD, should learn to collaborate, interact, and share space with peers effectively.

❏ Yes ❏ No

I section the classroom into specific learning areas (such as reading center, writing area, and math table).

❏ Yes ❏ No

Each area is labeled, and I have clearly defined the expectations for each center.

❏ Yes ❏ No

I have an area for whole class discussion and instruction.

❏ Yes ❏ No

I use this area for movement learning as well.

❏ Yes ❏ No

I rarely hang decorations or displays from light fixtures. I know this is a distraction for students.

❏ Yes ❏ No

I have a calming area for students to visit when they feel overwhelmed. This area is quiet and contains toys and activities to reduce anxiety.

❏ Yes ❏ No

If a student with ASD seems distracted by a school-related item (for instance, computers or phones), I keep these items in an area that is blocked from the student's view.

❏ Yes ❏ No

Building a Caring Classroom Community

To create a caring classroom community, teachers must be aware and sensitive to the thoughts and feelings of students with and without disabilities. It is important that every child believe that she is a functioning and contributing member of the class. Teachers can communicate this message to all children through words and actions.

Building a caring classroom might begin with these approaches:

- **Talk about differences.** Younger students may be unfamiliar with ASD and may be confused or frustrated when interacting with a peer with the disorder. High-quality picture books can be particularly helpful to prompt discussions about many types of differences. Take the time to explain that every child thinks and learns in different ways. Find ways to highlight and celebrate each child's strengths. Teach all students to show pride in their accomplishments.

- **Use team-building language.** Begin the school year referring to your classroom as a team. Discuss explicitly how students can help one another learn. Incorporate daily activities that allow students to work cooperatively.

- **Intervene when children are teased or bullied.** Make sure every student knows that it is never acceptable to tease peers. Discourage students from laughing at a classmate's weaknesses or mistakes.

- **Model ways to support students with ASD.** Show students how they can help their classmates without doing tasks for them. Find ways that your students with ASD can support and encourage their peers too. All students should feel like a part of the classroom community.

- **Encourage all students to participate.** Carefully plan lessons so that each child has many opportunities to participate in learning. Differentiate learning assignments so that all children can experience success daily.

Designing and Maintaining Classroom Routines

Students with ASD thrive in structured environments. When their daily routines become unpredictable, students can become frustrated and upset. Such feelings of anxiousness can lead to disruptive behavior. As a result, it is important that students with ASD are intensely aware of classroom routines and have ample warning when class schedules change.

A classroom visual schedule can be a valuable tool for many students in the classroom. Label and order picture cards for class activities for each day in a common learning area. Review class schedules daily with the class during a morning meeting. Additionally, make sure to review changes to regularly scheduled events.

Students who require more control over their daily schedules can use individual daily schedules. Individual schedules are smaller versions of the classroom visual schedule that allow students to view the order of class activities and remove or cover tasks from the schedule card when they are completed.

Transitions are a significant aspect of classroom routines as well. Students with ASD need to know when activities begin or end, and they also need to be able to anticipate changes to the schedule. This is where the visual schedule helps. Being unable to complete a task can be extremely frustrating to some students with ASD. Consequently, teachers must have multiple transition plans in place.

Consider these ideas for primary student transition plans:

- Use manipulatives to count down to the end of a task. Begin an activity with a manipulative for each time interval (for instance, one cube for each five-minute period). Take away a cube after each interval.

- Set a timer to account for the time period of each task. Consider using timers with visual signals, as buzzers or bells can be distracting.

- Prepare children when a task will be coming to an end soon. Tell the child when it is five minutes, two minutes, and one minute before the end of a task or activity.

- For students who are able to read a clock, communicate the activity start and end times. Add clock faces with activity start and stop times to classroom or individual visual schedules.

- Use music or another pleasant sound (such as chimes) to signal the close of an activity. Students can sing a transition song with the teacher or the teacher can play transition music.

Strategies to Help Include Learners with ASD

Four Corners Favorites
Why Use This Strategy?
Typically developing students are often curious about their peers with disabilities. However, young students may not know how to begin to engage with students with ASD.

Although it is natural for students to notice differences in the classroom setting, it can be more difficult for students to see similarities. Four Corners Favorites provides all students with an opportunity to explore common interests between themselves and others.

How Does This Strategy Work?

- Design a series of age-appropriate personal-interest questions. Be sure that each question has four possible responses. (For example: What is your favorite ice cream? Chocolate, vanilla, strawberry, or peanut butter?)

- Assign each response a corner in the classroom.

- Have students move to the corner in the classroom that represents their response.

- After each question, ask at least one student to share the reason for selecting that response.

Teacher Tips

- Set expectations for this activity. Be sure students understand that they must walk to classroom corners, pay attention to questions and response choices, and listen to the responses of others.

Sample Questions and Responses

- What do you like to do after school? (ride a bike, play video games, listen to music, or read)

- In what season is your birthday? (fall, winter, spring, or summer)

- What subject do you like best in school? (math, reading, writing, or science)

- What is your favorite lunch food? (pizza, hot dogs, tacos, or chicken)

- What is your favorite area of a playground? (slide, swings, monkey bars, or sandbox)

- What sport do you like best? (baseball, basketball, dance, or hockey)

- Encourage students to make choices based on their own likes and dislikes. Discourage students from imitating the responses of peers.

- Assign the center of the room as a place to indicate a favorite not represented by the other four choices. After each question, encourage the students in the center of the room to share their choices aloud.

- For very large classes, consider having the children answer the questions in smaller groups. For example, girls could answer first, followed by boys, or students could respond by table groups.

- Ask students to submit questions they would like the class to answer. Help students design questions with four responses.

- After the activity, discuss similarities among the group (for example, most of the class likes chocolate ice cream best or no one in our classroom has a spring birthday).

- Take note of common interests among groups of students. This information can be helpful for partner or group pairing for future activities or projects.

- If a student with ASD needs assistance with this activity, consider pairing the child with a responsible classmate or adult aide. Encourage the student to make a verbal choice before moving to a corner to indicate a response.

Relevant IFSP or IEP Goals

Consider whether or not the following goals might be appropriate for students with ASD who are participating in a game of Four Corners Favorites.

- Preschool—Given a visual choice of two objects, student will indicate a want by pointing to the desired object in three out of four opportunities.

- Kindergarten—Student will indicate a preference or interest in response to *wh-* questions with two or more answer choices in three out of four opportunities with prompts or cues.

- First or second grade—Student will indicate a preference or interest in response to *wh-* questions in three out of four opportunities with prompts or cues.

Schoolwide Scavenger Hunt
Why Use This Strategy?

- Sometimes it is necessary that the school community work together to support a student with ASD. This means that staff members beyond the child's individual classroom teacher must be familiar with the child and her individual needs.

- Building relationships with students with ASD takes time and planning. A Schoolwide Scavenger Hunt helps students with ASD become familiar with important spaces in the school and helpful personnel throughout the building.

How Does This Strategy Work?

- Design clues about important spaces in the school building (such as the school office, library, or nurse's office).

- Place clues in each appropriate space throughout the school building. Keep in mind that each clue will indicate the next space to which the children will travel, rather than the space they are in currently.

- In a large group, read the clues to students. Solicit their guesses about where to go next.

- Follow each clue until the scavenger hunt is complete. Discuss the places and the people students met during the hunt.

Sample Scavenger Hunt Clues

1. Where we start is a busy place,
   It's where we see our secretary's smiling face.
   In this place there's plenty to do,
   And the principal works here often too. (school office)

2. Our second stop can be loud,
   It's where you'll see a student crowd.
   And if you're hungry and want to munch,
   Come in here to eat your lunch. (cafeteria)

3. Coming next is where we play.
   There are slides and swings for a sunny day.
   When we're done, we line up to go in.
   And learning time will begin again. (recess area)

4. If outside you trip or fall,
   Get sick at school and or hit with a ball.
   There's never a need to yell or yelp,
   Find this place and ask for help. (nurse's station)

Teacher Tips

- Younger students who are less familiar with school may not have prior knowledge about some of its special spaces. Spend time before or after this activity explaining more information about what happens in each special place in the school and who is available to help in those areas.

- Consider inviting one or more school helpers to visit your classroom later in the school year. Allow students to interview them about their work at the school.

- Emphasize the qualities of each special helper's job in a positive way. For example, stress that the principal's main responsibility is to keep students safe, rather than to discipline.

- During the first weeks of school, continue to reinforce the location of special places in the school as well as the names of the teachers and staff who work there.

Relevant IFSP or IEP Goals

Consider whether or not the following goals might be appropriate for children with ASD who are participating in the school-wide scavenger hunt activity.

- Preschool—Student will identify correctly the name of her classroom teacher without prompts or cues.

- Kindergarten—Student will identify correctly the name and job of familiar school personnel in two out of three opportunities with visual prompts or cues.

- First or second grade—Student will request assistance from appropriate school personnel in two out of three opportunities with visual prompts or cues.

All about Us Class Book
Materials
11" x 14" pieces of poster board or construction paper
Pictures from home

Why Use This Strategy?
During the first few weeks of school, it can be difficult to get to know students with ASD. This is especially true if students' communication skills are delayed. Using this home

learning project, teachers can gather information about students' likes and dislikes relatively quickly.

Throughout the school year, both the teacher and students can use this book to recall details about individual students in the class. Teachers can use students' specific interests to develop differentiated learning or to plan class rewards.

How Does This Strategy Work?

- Give each student a piece of 11" x 14" poster board or construction paper.

- Instruct students to add photos or magazine pictures of their favorite activities, sports, foods, games, and so on. Send home a note outlining the project to families. (A sample letter follows.)

- Combine student pages to create a book.

Sample Family Letter

Dear Families,

My students and I are making a book, and we need your help!

Each student is writing his/her own page in a book all about us. Each page should have a title—All about [insert child's name]!—written horizontally at the top of the paper.

Below the title, students should include information about themselves. Students can write themselves or dictate their ideas to a family member. Here are some suggested sentence starters for your child's page:

I am ___ years old.

I like to _____.

I am good at _____.

My favorite (sport, game, book, and so on) is _____.

I have _____ brothers and sisters.

I want to be a _____ when I grow up.

I can _____.

I feel happy when _____.

Your student should also decorate his/her page with drawings, photographs, or magazine pictures that tell more about their writing. Please note that these pages may be laminated, and pictures and photographs included on pages will not be returned.

All pages are due _____. On this day, students will be asked to share their pages with their classmates before we combine the pages into a class book.

Thank you for helping us as we grow into a class community!

Sincerely,

Teacher Tips

- Before assembling the book, allow students to share their pages with their peers. Help students see similarities in interests among their classmates.

- Consider laminating each student page to make the book more durable.

- Don't forget to create your own teacher page for the book. Students want to know about you too! This page can also be an example for students to reference before making their own pages.

- Add the book to a classroom library. Students will enjoy sharing the book during reading time.

- Attach student pages with two large metal binder rings. This makes book reassembly easy when new students join the class. Similarly, the book can be easily dismantled at the end of the school year so that pages can be returned to students as a keepsake.

- If a child does not produce a page with his family, set aside class time to complete the page at school. All students should be highlighted in the class book.

Relevant IFSP or IEP Goals

Consider whether or not the following goals might be appropriate for children with ASD who are working to create an *All about Us* class book.

- Preschool—Student will identify correctly his first name in an array of other names with two or fewer prompts.

- Kindergarten—Student will identify correctly his street address and phone number with 100 percent accuracy in eight out of ten opportunities.

- First or second grade—Student will answer correctly in four out of five consecutive personal questions with two or fewer prompts.

Classroom Time Line

Materials
Construction paper or sentence strips
Marker
Sticky notes

Why Use This Strategy?
Similar to a time line of a historical figure, a classroom time line keeps a record of important and memorable classroom events and accomplishments. Recognizing individual and class achievements helps promote a sense of community.

When included in a general education classroom only partially, children with ASD may not always feel like or be treated as genuine members of their classes. A classroom time line acknowledges many different types of school success and encourages students to support and celebrate peers.

How Does This Strategy Work?

- Using sentence strips or construction paper cut into long strips, create a continuous line along one wall of the classroom.

- Divide the paper time line into equally spaced sections labeled with each school month.

- Commemorate individual or class accomplishments by writing them on sticky notes. See the sample ideas for time line celebrations that follow.

- Add the note to the time line in the appropriate space. Continue to add to the time line throughout the school year.

Sample Time Line Celebrations

Birthdays	New Students	School Concerts
Lost Teeth	Class Rewards	Mastered Skills
School Plays	Class Pets	School Awards
Student of the Week	100th Day of School	Sport Goals

Teacher Tips

- As often as possible, recognize class goals and accomplishments. This helps establish a team-like atmosphere in the classroom.

- Whenever possible, use theme shaped paper or self-made cutouts to showcase goals on the time line. For example, use a tooth shape for lost teeth or a sneaker for a sport goal. These symbols will help make the time line accessible to prereaders in the classroom.

- Always check with a student before adding his accomplishment to the time line. Some students may be embarrassed or reluctant to share their successes with others.

- Design or search the Internet for a short class cheer or chant to use when an achievement is added to the time line. Song and movement will help students with ASD establish the activity as a class routine.

Relevant IFSP or IEP Goals

Consider whether or not the following goals might be appropriate for children with ASD who are helping to create the classroom time line.

- Preschool—Given two picture prompts in a sequence, the student will identify the picture that shows what happened first in three out of four opportunities.

- Kindergarten—In four out of five opportunities, a student will sequence correctly three pictures with one prompt or none.

- First or second grade—Student will identify what happened first, next, and last in a past event with no more than three visual or verbal teacher prompts.

A Day in the Life of Our Class
Materials
Paper
Photographs
Glue or tape

Why Use This Strategy?
Routine is very important to students with ASD. When daily activities are scheduled, learners with ASD feel less anxious and more focused. Routines also help reinforce teacher expectations for students' behavior and performance. All of these aspects better prepare students with ASD to complete tasks.

Visual supports can be helpful reminders of routines for students with ASD. This strategy allows all students to participate in creating a visual schedule that features the daily class activities.

How Does This Strategy Work?

- Take photographs of students doing daily class activities (saying the pledge of allegiance, doing math work, eating lunch, and so on). There should be one photograph for each significant activity during the school day.

- Give each student one photograph. Have each child write or dictate a one- to two-sentence caption for his assigned photograph.

- Glue each photograph and its caption on a separate piece of paper.

- Order the photographs with captions in a linear fashion to show the daily class routine.

Teacher Tips

- Wait at least two weeks after the start of the school year to begin this project. Schedules change frequently during the first few days of school.

- If possible, find a permanent place to display the visual schedule. That way, students can reference it throughout the school year. It also makes it easier for substitute teachers to maintain the established routine.

- Once displayed, make sure that the schedule has some flexibility of activity order or times. Remind students that even well-established schedules must change occasionally.

- Try to feature one student alone in every photograph. Using the names of the student in the photograph can help students with ASD recognize and use their peers' names.

- Pre-writers can dictate their sentences to a teacher. You can also use sentence starters to assist developing writers.

- Help children make a video entitled "A Day in the Life of Our Class" so that new students can be oriented to the routines.

Relevant IFSP or IEP Goals

Consider whether or not the following goals might be appropriate for children with ASD who are participating in the A Day in the Life of Our Class activity.

- Preschool—Given a description of the event, the student will correctly identify the photo that shows the event in four out of five opportunities with two or fewer prompts.

- Kindergarten—Given a photograph, the student will state verbally at least two details about what is shown with two or fewer prompts.

- First or second grade—Given a photograph, the student will provide at least two written details about what is shown.

How Do I Help?

Why Use This Strategy?

Students usually recognize differences among their peers with disabilities quickly. Young children want to be helpful to their teachers and classmates; however, many primary students do not know how to support their classmates with ASD without guidance.

The How Do I Help game gives students an opportunity to brainstorm ways they can support their classmates. This strategy also allows the teacher to discuss how to approach students who need assistance and how to help all students feel included.

How Does This Strategy Work?

- Have students sit in a circle in a sharing area in the classroom.

- Read a description of a classroom situation in which a student might need assistance.

- Ask students to discuss ways they could be helpful in the described situation.

- Continue the game with a new classroom situation.

Teacher Tips

- Whenever possible, gently guide students to appropriate responses. This technique allows

Sample Situations

- Julie is at recess. You hear some of the other children talking about her green shoes. They are laughing and pointing at her. How do you help?

- Mike feels sad because he cannot play the computer today. He is sitting at his desk by himself. You and your friends are playing a game. How do you help?

- The teacher asks you to read with Joey today. Joey is trying very hard, but can't read all of the words in his book. How do you help?

- Sara begins to cry because she broke her red crayon. Now she cannot color her fire truck picture. How do you help?

students to have more ownership in the idea, increasing the likelihood of use.

- Include at least one situation during the game that requires teacher intervention. Make sure that students understand that the adults at the school should be consulted immediately if any student feels sick, hurt, or threatened.

- Record some of students' ideas on a piece of poster board. Hang the chart in the classroom and reference it before cooperative activities.

- During the first few months of school, maintain a token jar to keep track of class helpfulness. Add a marble or button to the jar when students help their classmates appropriately. Plan a class reward when the jar is filled.

Relevant IFSP or IEP Goals

Consider whether or not the following goals might be appropriate for children with ASD who are learning to use the How Do I Help Strategy.

- Preschool—When requesting to leave her seat, student will raise her hand to ask teacher permission when given a verbal prompt.

- Kindergarten—Student will raise her hand to ask or answer a question given a visual prompt at least twice per school day.

- First or second grade—Without prompting, the student will raise her hand to ask or answer a question during class at least twice per school day.

The Superstar Bag
Materials
Paper bags
Items from home

Why Use This Strategy?
The Superstar Bag is a show-and-tell activity that allows students to practice peer-to-peer conversation. It also allows students to find out more about their classmates' interests.

This strategy addresses two common challenges for students with ASD: communication and social interaction. Using high-interest topics, students can concentrate on the mechanics of conversation, such as taking turns, maintaining focus, and asking questions.

How Does This Strategy Work?

- Give each student a small paper bag. Have each child take the bag home and fill it with three to four small items that tell about himself. See the sample letter to families.

- Ask students to return the filled bags to school.

- Place students in pairs. Have students take turns sharing items in their bags with their partners.

- Have each student report one new piece of information she learned about her partner to the class. (For example: "I learned that Mary's favorite color is orange." "I learned that Robert likes to play with trucks.")

Teacher Tips

- Help students recognize similarities in special items. Make note of common interests for future cooperative learning tasks.

- Model the activity for students by bringing in your own superstar bag. Allow students to ask you questions about your interests.

- Allow students who do not complete the assignment to borrow classroom objects for their bags. Make sure that every child participates in the activity.

- Support students who are nervous or anxious about sharing. Sit beside these students as they share and offer prompting to assist them as they tell about their objects.

Relevant IFSP or IEP Goals

Consider whether or not the following goals might be appropriate for children with ASD who are participating in the Superstar Bag strategy.

- Preschool—Student will correctly answer yes or no questions about himself when given visual prompts.

- Kindergarten—Given visual prompts, student will share one statement about himself with teachers or peers.

- First or second grade—With teacher prompting and visual prompts, student will share three statements about himself with a peer.

Read-Aloud Mini-Lessons
Why Use This Strategy?

- Under special circumstances, teachers may want to talk directly to students about autism. Explaining a highly complex disorder with technical terms, however, is not appropriate for young students.

Sample Superstar Bag Family Letter

Dear Families,

Our class is learning that we are special and we all are SUPERSTARS!

This week, we are sharing some of our favorite things with our classmates. Please help your child fill the attached bag with three to four small items that tell about him/her. For instance, you might include a yellow crayon because that is a favorite color or a block because your child likes to build. Be creative in your selections, but please do not send expensive or fragile items.

Children should bring their bags to school on _____. Each child will share his/her bag with a classmate, so be sure he/she can explain why he/she chose each item.

Thank you for helping us to learn a little more about your child!

Sincerely,

- There are many well-written, illustrated books that discuss ASD in child-friendly terms. These texts can help you lead a discussion about autism within the classroom.

How Does This Strategy Work?

- Select a book about ASD appropriate for your students' age group. If you need ideas, see the list that follows.

- Preview the book by sharing three to four of the illustrations. Ask students to make predictions about what the characters are doing or how the characters might be feeling.

- Read the story, stopping at appropriate points to monitor students' comprehension and to ask or answer questions.

- Solicit students' reactions to the story. Discuss ways that they could be a friend to a student like the character with ASD in the story.

Suggested ASD Picture Book Titles
for Pre-K to Second Grade
Bishop, Beverly. 2011. *My Friend with Autism.* Enhanced Edition. Arlington, TX: Future Horizons.

Written by a parent of a child with ASD, this book explains some of the behaviors of students with ASD that can be confusing to their peers. This updated version of the book includes a CD of accompanying coloring pages for young students.

Demonia, Lori. 2012. *Leah's Voice.* San Antonio, TX: Halo Publishing International.

Being the sibling of a child with ASD can be difficult. This book tells how one sister manages this experience.

Doering Tourville, Amanda. 2010. *My Friend Has Autism.* Mankato, MN: Picture Window Books.

Featuring multicultural characters, this book shows how two young boys become friends. Despite the fact that one boy has autism, the two boys like many of the same things and have fun together.

Edwards, Andreanna. 2002. *Taking Autism to School.* Valley Park, MO: JayJo Books.

This book explains autism in a child-friendly way. The book offers teachers suggestions for how to use it as a read-aloud and includes a student quiz to help reinforce concepts for young readers.

Ellis, Marvie. 2005. *Keisha's Doors: An Autism Story/Las Puertas de Keisha: Una Historia de Autismo.* Austin, TX: Speech Kids Texas Press.

Monica is frustrated with her little sister Keisha, who will not play with her. She later learns that her sister has autism. Written in both Spanish and English, this story shows how to demonstrate acceptance.

Ely, Lesley. 2004. *Looking After Louis.* Park Ridge, IL: Albert Whitman.

Children learn that Louis, a child with ASD, is not so different from them when he begins to play soccer. Colorful illustrations make this book fun and engaging.

Lears, Laurie. 1998. *Ian's Walk: A Story about Autism.* Park Ridge, IL: Albert Whitman.

The way that Julie experiences a walk to the park and the way that her brother experiences it are very different. In this book, we learn the ways that autism shapes how Ian sees the world around him.

Robinson Peete, Holly, and Ryan Elizabeth Peete. 2010. *My Brother Charlie.* New York: Scholastic.

Ryan loves her twin brother Charlie even though he has autism. This book shares many of the positive aspects of having a brother with ASD.

Shally, Celeste. 2012. *Since We're Friends: An Autism Picture Book.* New York: Sky Pony Press.

Making friends with a child with autism is not easy, but it can be very rewarding. This book explains how one child shows compassion to a peer with the disability.

Teacher Tips

- Never discuss an individual child's diagnosis with students in the classroom. This information should remain private unless parents grant permission.

- Preview any book on ASD that you decide to share. Be sure that it is appropriate for the developmental level of your students.

- Keep copies of the books you share in the reading area in the classroom. Students may want to reread them or ask additional questions.

Relevant IFSP or IEP Goals

Consider whether or not the following goals might be appropriate for children with ASD who are participating in the class discussions using books.

- Preschool—When hearing a narrative story read aloud, the student will name correctly who the story is about with one or fewer visual prompts.

- Kindergarten—When hearing a narrative story read aloud and being given a visual prompt, the student will name correctly how a story character is feeling in two or more places in the story.

- First or second grade—When hearing a narrative story read aloud and being given a verbal sentence prompt, the student will state the main idea (what the story is about) in three out of five opportunities.

Technology Resources for Including Students with ASD

- Look on the web for getting-to-know-you questions for children (https://www.thegamegal.com/2013/10/18/get-to-know-you-questions/) and general conversation starters for students (http://slplearningcurve.blogspot.com/2010/06/getting-to-know-you-questions-for-kids.html).

- Positively Autism (http://positivelyautism.weebly.com) offers many free resources to help build social, academic, and behavior skills in school and at home.

- Help students with ASD become familiar with the school environment with several school-themed scavenger hunt ideas and templates at Quick Hunts (http://www.quickhunts.com/).

- Showcase similarities among students by having them create all-about-me books (http://printables.atozteacherstuff.com/420/all-about-me-printable-book/) or all-about-me crafts (http://www.dltk-kids.com/crafts/miscellaneous/all_about_me.htm).

- Voice Thread, which costs about $15 per month (http://voicethread.com/) can be used to enhance all-about-me class projects. This software allows users to embed audio comments into documents, presentations, images, and videos.

- Visit the Professional Learning Board (https://k12teacherstaffdevelopment.com/tlb/how-can-i-use-a-timeline-in-the-classroom-as-a-creative-learning-tool/) for creative ways to use time lines in the classroom.

- Use ASD children's book lists on the web (http://www.autism-resources.com/books-children.html or http://www.todaysparent.com/blogs/special-needs-parenting/15-best-books-about-autism) to select stories that will help students better understand their classmates with ASD.

- The Teaching Community (http://teaching .monster.com/benefits/articles/8761–22 -tips-for-teaching-students-with-autism -spectrum-disorders) has several quick tips to help teach students with ASD.

- Paula Kluth, ASD author and advocate, outlines many easy-to-implement strategies for creating an inclusive classroom environment on her blog (http://www .paulakluth.com/).

Key Terms

impulsive behavior: Actions with little thought or regard to others.

inclusion: The acceptance of students with disabilities in general education classrooms with appropriate services and supports for varying amounts of time, depending on needs.

interventions: Strategies or techniques used in the classroom to help students whose behavior, skills, or understanding have limited their progress through more common practices.

noncompliance: Refusal to follow directives.

perseverative behavior: The repetition of a behavior without obvious practical reason.

self-injurious behavior: Behaviors that cause harm to oneself purposefully.

self-stimulatory behaviors/stimming/stims: Another term for perseverative behaviors, indicating behaviors that may attempt to affect levels of sensory stimulation.

sensory hypersensitivity: Anxiety or stress caused from oversensitivity to one's environment.

sensory hyposensitivity: Anxiety or stress caused from under-sensitivity to one's environment; may cause a need to seek additional sensory stimulation from other sources.

3 Strengthening Their Voices: Facilitating Functional Communication

Mrs. Clark's kindergarten class is celebrating Emma's sixth birthday. As a special treat, Emma has brought in birthday cupcakes decorated with pink frosting and rainbow sprinkles. Students wait anxiously as Emma and Mrs. Clark open the box of cupcakes. While Mrs. Clark holds the large box, Emma walks from student to student asking each child to choose his favorite, chocolate or vanilla. Eventually, Emma comes to Luke, a student with ASD. "Chocolate or vanilla?" Emma asks. Luke just stares at the box of treats. A little louder this time, Emma says, "Chocolate or vanilla, Luke?" There is still no reply. Mrs. Clark intervenes, "Luke, do you like chocolate or vanilla cupcakes?" Luke responds, "Chocolate or vanilla?" Tired of waiting for Luke to decide, Emma gives Luke a chocolate cupcake. Luke immediately begins to eat. As he hurries, his face becomes covered with pink frosting. Nearby students start to giggle. Noticing the mess, Mrs. Clark calls Luke over to the sink in the classroom. When Luke arrives, Mrs. Clark uses a mirror to show Luke the frosting on his face. Both Mrs. Clark and Luke begin to giggle now too. "Come on, Luke," Mrs. Clark says, "Let's wash that face off." Immediately, Luke's face changes from joyful to terrified. He runs back to his desk, crawls beneath it, and covers his face with his hands. A worried Mrs. Clark follows behind him, questioning, "What's wrong, Luke?" Through his tear-stained face, Luke cries out, "No wash face off! No wash face off! Face stay on! Face stay on!" At first, Luke's teacher was totally surprised by his response, but now it all makes sense.

Purpose of Communication

Communication is the use of speech, text, or gestures to exchange information. When communication is effective, people are connected through a shared understanding of ideas. This type of interaction allows people to meet their needs and to form relationships with others. Conversely, deficits in communication, like some of the characteristics of ASD, can restrict social growth and school progress. This is why it is so important that classroom teachers implement strategies to support language development in students with ASD.

In the example described in the opening of the chapter, Luke has problems understanding and being understood by his teacher and classmates. For example, Emma wants him to select a cupcake, but Luke only repeats the question, and Emma loses patience. Similarly, Luke is confused when he is asked to "wash his face off." Luke takes it literally and, in order to avoid it, he runs and hides. To a person who does not understand pervasive developmental disorders, Luke's responses in both of these social interactions might be interpreted as defiance rather than confusion.

So how might a teacher intervene to help Luke in this classroom situation? The answer begins by understanding some general communication strengths and needs of students with ASD. Many students with ASD think and plan visually. Showing the two choices while asking Luke to select his favorite kind of cupcake would be helpful. In addition, many students with ASD are literal thinkers; figurative language is difficult to comprehend. With this knowledge, Mrs. Clark could have selected her words more carefully. "Let's wash the *frosting* off of your face" or simply "Let's wash your face" may have communicated more clearly to Luke.

Language is an extraordinary part of social development. It helps us to share our wants and needs and to bond with others around us.

Communicating well with others is also critical to long-term productivity and independence. With an abundance of social partners, the classroom community is the ideal place to practice and strengthen speech and language skills. For many students with ASD, effective communication begins with functional language.

Functional and Nonfunctional Language

One of the greatest challenges of students with ASD is communicating functionally. Functional communication holds shared meaning for both the speaker and the receiver. For instance, the teacher asks Traci what she would like for lunch. She replies, "hot dog." This is an example of functional communication. The teacher asked Traci a question. Traci processed the question and replied with a response that was meaningful to both her and the teacher.

Nonfunctional communication, however, does not hold mutual understanding for the speaker and receiver even though the words may be expressed properly. Once again, the teacher asks Traci what she would like for lunch. This time Traci replies, "Triangle, circles." Traci has provided an answer; she wants pepperoni pizza—a triangle with circles. In this instance, Traci processed the question, but replied with a response that holds meaning only to her.

Although nonfunctional communication may be confusing to classroom teachers, it is often meaningful to the student. Accordingly, teachers need to approach these efforts at communication as intriguing puzzles that will help them to better understand the child. Daily observations, surveys of students' interests, and input from families can help teachers better understand what students with ASD are trying to communicate through nonfunctional speech. Once shared meaning is achieved, teachers should validate the student's efforts and model a more functional response. In the lunch example described above, when Traci's teacher figures out that "triangle, circles" means pepperoni pizza, she might elaborate on Traci's ideas with a comment such as, "You're right—a slice of pizza does have a triangle and circles. I think you want pepperoni pizza. Please tell me you want pepperoni pizza for lunch today." Over time, through this gentle "nudging," Traci's speech moves in the direction of becoming more functional, and she is better able to communicate her needs and wants.

Expressive and Receptive Communication

Communication is often thought of as what is said, but it also includes what is heard and understood. Expressive language is the use of words to communicate. Rules of syntax, however, regulate language and give meaning to ideas. Verb tense, word use, and sentence structure are all important to build effective communication. These rules give meaning to collections of words (such as *I have a little blue car* rather than *blue I car has a little*).

In contrast, receptive communication is the language that is processed and understood. Receptive language is what allows children to follow directions and build language comprehension. Because of their ties to personal safety and socialization, these skills make receptive language equally as important as expressive language. Yet receptive language develops internally and is much more difficult to evaluate.

Throughout childhood, both receptive and expressive language develop, but receptive language typically grows more quickly. The number of words young children hear far exceeds those that they use independently. As Lars Staehr noted in his article titled "Vocabulary Size and the Skills of Listening, Reading, and Writing," young children's receptive language can be as much as four times more advanced than their expressive language. However, receptive and expressive language may be delayed in children with ASD because they are often less engaged than other children with the adults and peers using language around them, as researcher Rhiannon Luyster and her colleagues found in their studies.

Receptive, Expressive, or Both?

Read the following examples of classroom activities. Decide whether the task requires language skills that are receptive, expressive, or both.

1. Mr. Smith tells Joseph to point to the red apple.

2. Mason tells his teacher he is hungry.

3. April asks to use the restroom.

4. The teacher asks Gregory to answer questions about the story she just read to him.

5. Mrs. King asks Nick to write his name on the top of his paper.

6. The teacher asks Debra to recite the date.

7. Miss Jones asks the class to take out a pencil.

Answers
1. receptive; 2. expressive; 3. expressive; 4. both; 5. receptive; 6. both; and 7. receptive.

Echolalia and Scripting

Students with ASD may use echolalia and scripting to communicate. When a child repeats a word or phrase, this is called echolalia. For example, when the teacher says, "Go to the listening center," the student replies "Go to the listening center." Essentially, the child is echoing the words she has heard. Echolalia, however, can be delayed. For instance, two days later, the teacher asks the student what she likes about school, and she replies, "Go to the listening center."

Although it may seem nonfunctional, echolalia can be valuable. Through echolalia, students with ASD learn speech patterns that can be transferred to new situations. Additionally, echolalia can carry a functional message. In the example described above, the student was asked what she likes about school. Her reply, "Go to the listening center," could communicate that the listening center is an activity she prefers. Asking for clarification with the question, "Is the listening center your favorite part of school?" could give meaning to the student's words.

Scripting is a specific type of delayed echolalia. Scripting usually is a repeated word or phrase, often from television, music, or movies. For example, after watching a commercial for a cell phone, a student may repeat the words "from the palm of your hand to around the world." In the following weeks, the child may continue to repeat that phrase in his speech or use it to respond to others. For instance, when asked what he wants to do, the child says, "from the palm of your hand to around the world" to indicate that he wants to call a friend.

In addition to functional ideas, scripting can communicate feelings. Scripting helps some children with ASD cope with high anxiety. When a child scripts, he may be communicating, "I am overwhelmed," or, "I don't understand what to do." Repeating words or phrases can have a calming effect on students, and may be so integral to daily functioning that some children may be unaware that they are scripting. Monitoring when and how often students with ASD tend to script can help teachers recognize potential stressors for individual students.

Some students with ASD use echolalia when they are anxious or frustrated. Encourage students to use pictures, signs, or signals to communicate when they are too overwhelmed to use words.

If students with ASD do not know how to respond to a question or statement, they may use scripting. Teach students to use "I don't know" when they are confused. When possible, prompt students with responses to help them answer correctly.

When asking questions with multiple responses, switch the order of the responses to verify the child's response. For example, the teacher asks Shay, "Do you want red or blue paint?" Shay responds, "Blue paint." So the teacher asks Shay, "Do you want blue paint or red paint?" If Shay responds "blue paint" again, she has probably understood the question and is not using echolalia.

Keep in mind that both scripting and echolalia are forms of communication. Take the time to study how students with ASD might be using this language to express themselves.

Social Communication Concerns

ASD can influence social interaction profoundly. Delays in social communication can affect how students with ASD interpret and respond to social cues. Without these complex skills, building and maintaining friendships can be difficult. When teachers are able to recognize the ways ASD affects social communication, they are better able to support students within the classroom. See table 3.1 describing common social communication problems for students with ASD and suggested strategies for addressing these concerns.

Table 3.1   Common Social Communication Problems for Students with ASD

Communication Problem	Example	Strategy Suggestions
Topic Perseveration	George likes tigers. Whenever he is with peers, he talks only about tigers, their habitats, and their lifestyles. George's peers begin to avoid him at lunch.	• Set time limits for topics. • Explore other interests. • Use signals to help students know when to change topics.
	First grader Shania is captivated by a children's television program that includes unicorns. She has Asperger syndrome and is exceptionally articulate. During sharing time, she talks about her unicorn. "Shania's lying," one child says. "Yeah, she never did that stuff," another says.	Provide functional outlets for sharing both fantasy ideas (story writing, role-play, dress-up, and so on) and real information (reports, class projects, artwork of unicorns and other mythical creatures, and so on).
Interpreting Slang and Figurative Language	The teacher tells Susan the homework is "a piece of cake." Susan asks the teacher if she can have cookies instead.	• Explain the confusing word or phrase. • Practice using the word or phrase in context.
	Shayla and the teacher's aide are looking for the salamander that lives in the classroom. Suddenly, Shayla begins to cry. When Shayla could not locate the animal, the aide had said, "It's right there. If it were any closer, it would have bitten you."	• If possible, encourage the child to articulate her distress. • Explain the meaning of the phrase. • Pair the phrase in context with the simplified meaning. (For example, "It's right there. If it were any closer, it would have bitten you. That means that it's so close, you could touch it.")
Reading Facial Expressions	Whenever it is circle time and children are about to play a game, Anita says "doggie" over and over again because she wants that role. A classmate says, "That's not fair!" and several others agree.	• Encourage the child to draw or describe how her face might look if she were in her classmate's position. • Make connections between situational events and expressed feelings. (For example, "When I don't get a turn, I feel sad.")
	Henry got a new toy train for his birthday last month. He tells his classmates about it every day at lunch even though their faces appear bored.	• Discuss the facial signs for common emotions (a frown for sad, a wide smile for surprised, and so on). • Practice decoding facial expressions in magazine photos.
Inferring Emotions	A three-year-old scraped his knee on the playground and needed a bandage. Now Jeanetta, his classmate with ASD, keeps pursuing him and pressing on the bandage because it has her favorite cartoon character on it.	• Discuss appropriate social responses to various situations (for example, sickness). • Practice inferring characters' emotions in age-appropriate literature.
	Nolan overhears a peer tell the teacher that his mother is in the hospital. Nolan rushes over to the peer to tell him facts about ambulances.	• Role-play appropriate responses to social situations. • Share age-appropriate video of positive social interaction.

Treating ASD Language Delays

Each student with ASD will have unique communication needs. Addressing speech concerns requires a combination of child-specific supports and services. Because specialized speech services are usually only a small portion of the school day, teachers must learn to support communication development within the inclusive classroom. Accordingly, it is critical that classroom teachers are aware of the speech and language resources and integrate them into their daily instructional practices.

Speech-Language Pathologists

A speech-language pathologist (SLP) works with students to expand functional communication. For students with ASD, sessions with an SLP can occur within the school setting, private outpatient services, or a combination of both. Although speech therapy in public schools is available at no cost to families, outpatient speech sessions usually require out-of-pocket payment or private insurance. Within school, students may have push-in speech sessions, which allow students to work toward goals in the classroom. Alternatively, they may have pull-out, one-to-one, or small-group sessions with the SLP.

SLPs assist students in at least one of three areas of deficit: articulation, fluency, and language. Articulation goals focus on improving the production of sounds, such as /th/ or /r/. Conversely, fluency goals concentrate more on smoothness and pace of speech. One of the most common speech fluency disorders is stuttering. Students with ASD, however, commonly have language goals that address how speech is spoken, processed, and understood.

Regardless of individual student goals, collaboration among SLPs and school staff is critical to the language development of students with ASD. Classroom teachers should be aware of speech IEP goals, and work with pathologists to design instruction that supports the student's language development. It is also helpful to plan for social communication practice throughout the school day. Discuss with SLPs how to use natural environments, such as the cafeteria, recess, or learning centers, to facilitate social language.

Augmentative and Alternative Communication

Sometimes students with ASD will need additional support to develop language skills. In these cases, augmentative and alternative communication (AAC) may be necessary. Excluding verbal speech, AAC describes every method of communication used to share information. Most typically developing children use AAC daily when they wave hello, draw a picture, or smile at friends. Yet for some students with ASD, AAC is the only way to communicate functionally.

There are many types of AAC that students with ASD can use in schools. Some forms are unaided, using the physical movement of the body to communicate ideas. Sign language is an example of unaided communication a student with ASD may use. Other forms of AAC are aided, which means they incorporate some type of tool to produce functional language. Some AAC devices, such as iPads, are equipped with software that allows them to be used for AAC, and other products are designed especially for communication use.

AAC can be simple or highly complex. These terms refer to the range of technology that the AAC uses. Simple AAC methods are nonelectronic; complex ones use more-advanced technology to produce verbal speech. Simple and complex AAC methods can vary greatly in size, function, and portability. The following examples identify some common methods of each type:

Simple AAC

- Picture cards
- Books
- Letter or message boards

Complex AAC

- Tablets
- Smart phones
- Computers
- Speech-generating devices, such as DynaVox

Teachers and caregivers should consider the abilities and needs of the individual with ASD carefully to determine appropriate AAC strategies for each child.

Sign Language

The English language is infused with meaningful gestures. Teachers commonly wave hello, place a finger to their lips to quiet a group, and shrug their shoulders to indicate uncertainty. Even when students with ASD have verbal skills, sign language can be an effective way to support communication. During times of overwhelming frustration, it can be difficult for students with ASD to express their needs and wants. Encouraging them to sign their feelings can help prevent behaviors from quickly escalating.

Teaching children with ASD to use sign language effectively, however, requires a great deal more thought and planning. Not only must teachers know how to select signs, but they also must know how to motivate students to use them.

Before signs are used in the classroom, teachers must carefully choose which signs to use. Incorporating too many signs too quickly can be confusing and overwhelming for young students, so introducing signs one or two at a time is best. Once students are comfortable using that sign, new signs can be added. Begin with signs that have frequent use in the class (help, more, please) because students will have many opportunities to practice the sign.

Once a sign is selected, introduce it in a novel way. This will capture the attention of students and make the sign memorable. For instance, read a book with frequent use of the word and encourage students to form the sign each time the word is said. Another idea is to sing a song with the word and encourage students to sign the word when the word is sung. Both of these activities pair the sign and word together in an engaging and functional way. Afterward, use the sign and word together as often as possible to help students learn to use the sign.

Tips to Remember When Using Sign Language

- Consider introducing signs to the whole class, rather than only to students with ASD. Young children are often interested in learning signs, and they can serve as models to students with ASD.

- Encourage students with ASD to use signs, but do not force them. Allow students to communicate in ways that make them most comfortable.

- Be aware that children may not use signs as precisely as adults. Acknowledge approximations.

- Continue to use other means of communication along with signs in the classroom. Help students with ASD build other verbal and nonverbal communication skills.

What Would You Do?

How might you adapt these typical school experiences to include students with ASD and non-verbal language?

- Your first-grade classroom is planning a play for Presidents' Day. Every student has a small speaking part. Leo, a student in your classroom, uses a speech-generating device.

- Tommy sits alone at his desk at recess. When you ask a group of children playing a board game to include Tommy, they say he can't play because he can't talk.

- It's show-and-tell day in kindergarten. Will has brought in his stuffed frog to show.

- During circle time, the class is learning a new song about friendship. Imani enjoys music and wants to participate with the class.

- The teacher asks each student to participate in calendar time. Every student answers a question about the month, day, or date. It's Joshua's turn to respond.

In each of these situations, students with nonverbal language can be included and can contribute. Here are some possible adaptations:

- In the school play, Leo could be taught to use his AAC to speak his lines. In a situation where an AAC is not available, this student could participate by holding scene or title cards for the audience to read.

- At recess, Tommy could be paired with a classmate to play the game. You could create a simple yes-or-no board to allow for some shared decision making during game play. Tommy could move the pieces while the other child shares the team's game choices.

- For show-and-share, the teacher could work with the family to help plan Will's presentation. Parents could provide some background information on the item that could be incorporated into the show-and-share. One way to do this is to use picture cards to show information about the stuffed frog. For example, Will could show his classmates a picture card for sleeping so that he could share that he sleeps with his frog each night. Then it would be up to the children to interpret the image and infer that Will sleeps with his stuffed toy frog each night.

- When the song is introduced, the teacher could incorporate several sign language signs. The teacher could encourage Imani and her peers to use the signs while the music plays. Alternatively, the teacher and students could work together to assign large body movements or hand motions to different parts of the song. All students could use the gestures to move with the music.

- The teacher could prepare a series of response cards for Joshua that coordinate to a specific question about the calendar. Joshua could show his answer to the question by pointing to or raising the correct response card. The teacher could provide immediate feedback or support to Joshua.

Students with Nonverbal Language

According to Kelly Stickles Goods and colleagues in a journal article, approximately 25 to 30 percent of preschool students with ASD have limited or no verbal speech. Limited speech does not necessarily indicate limited intellect. Although these students are nonverbal, they can learn to communicate. Many nonverbal students with ASD will learn to use gestures, sounds, sign language, symbols, or devices to communicate with others. Within the school community, teachers and support staff should be trained to support nonverbal students with ASD in the communication style that allows them to function best. The following are suggestions for how teachers can create an environment that fosters language development in nonverbal students.

- **Integrate signals into daily activities.** Design class-wide signals to transition between activities or to gain class attention. Build a sense of class community by encouraging all students to use class signals.

- **Decode nonverbal messages.** Physical movement, sounds, gestures, and even aggressive behaviors are all ways that nonverbal students with ASD may communicate. Observe the environment, the possible cause of the behavior, and the consequences of the student's actions to determine the intent of the child's message.

- **Inspire language.** Use students' interests to stimulate language development. Encourage students to communicate their wants and needs through a variety of methods that are comfortable for them.

- **Encourage participation.** Adapt assignments so that all students can contribute in the classroom. Allow students to use AAC to participate in activities that typically require speech.

- **Teach acceptance.** Model ways to include and interact with students with nonverbal language. Teach typically developing students to pay attention to students with nonverbal language, to seek to understand them, and not to talk for them.

- **Give students the time and space to express themselves.** Speak to students with nonverbal language as though you expect them to answer. Provide wait time for students to respond, and acknowledge verbal and nonverbal attempts to communicate.

- **Use respectful language.** Select words and a tone that are supportive, rather than condescending. Remember too, that students who are nonverbal can hear what is said about them and that a child with ASD often has developed stronger receptive language skills than expressive language skills.

When it comes to facilitating effective communication, time is the greatest asset. In a school year, language development may be gradual for many students with ASD. However, teachers who are patient and are supportive of students' goals will observe growth in functional communication. Interventions should include peer models and allow for daily opportunities to practice and experiment with language.

Strategies That Support Functional Communication

Teachers should make every effort to help students make the connection between language and shared understanding. The strategies in the following sections can help young students with ASD see the importance of this relationship.

The Roll a Response Strategy: A Small-Group Activity

Materials

Whiteboard or chart paper

Marker

Tennis ball (one for each pair)

Why Use This Strategy?

Even when students with ASD have verbal skills, they may find it difficult to make sense of the rules of social communication. Although school provides many opportunities for children to build social language, many young students with ASD will need additional support to interact functionally with their classmates.

The Roll a Response strategy offers students a concrete way to think about the structure of conversation. Pairing high-interest, child-friendly questions with physical activity, Roll a Response helps children with ASD understand conversational turn-taking. This strategy also provides authentic practice with language processing and expression.

How Does This Strategy Work?

- Generate a list of age-appropriate getting-to-know-you questions and write them on a whiteboard or on chart paper. Sample questions follow.

- Partner a student who has ASD with a typically developing peer. Tell students that they are going to practice asking and answering questions.

- Be sure that both children understand that conversation involves turn-taking. One person talks and another listens. Discuss what happens when both people talk (no one hears what is said).

- Assign roles to each partner. The student with ASD will be the responder first; the typically developing peer will be the questioner first.

- Give each pair one tennis ball.

- The questioner begins the activity by asking a getting-to-know-you question. After asking the question, the questioner rolls the ball to the responder. Then the responder answers the question and rolls the ball back to the questioner.

- The game continues with a new question.

- After students have had sufficient time for three to five question exchanges, partners reverse roles.

Teacher Tips

- Set clear expectations for this activity. Make sure that students understand how and when the ball should be handled.

- Help students understand that they may only talk when they have the ball in their

Sample Questions

- What is your favorite color (or game, animal, sport, food)?
- What television shows do you like?
- When is your bedtime?
- What do you like to do after school?
- What do you do in the summer?

- How many brothers or sisters do you have?
- When is your birthday?
- Where does your family go on vacation?
- How do you get to school each day?
- What is something fun you did this week?

Practical Strategies for Supporting Young Learners with Autism Spectrum Disorder

hand. The ball reminds them it is their turn to speak.

- During the first few exchanges, students with ASD and their peers will need a high level of support. Assist students in asking questions and communicating appropriate responses.

- As students become comfortable with this activity, try to add multiple exchanges with the same question. For instance, after a question is answered, a partner could pose a follow-up question. (For example: "Do you have a pet?" "What kind of pet do you have?").

- Encourage students to maintain eye contact during the question exchanges.

- You might consider covering the sides of a square box with different emoticons, one on each side. Have children roll the box as they would dice and then identify a situation that would match that emotion.

Relevant IFSP or IEP Goals

Consider whether or not the following goals might be appropriate for children with ASD who are participating in the Roll a Response activity.

- Preschool—Student will demonstrate appropriate turn-taking skills by waiting for her own turn during three out of five exchanges.

- Kindergarten—Student will demonstrate appropriate turn-taking skills by staying seated and waiting for her own turn during four out of five exchanges.

- First or second grade—Student will demonstrate appropriate turn-taking skills by staying seated, maintaining eye contact during a peer's turn, and waiting for her own turn during four out of five exchanges.

The Out of the Box Strategy: A One-on-One Activity
Materials
Small box (shoebox size)
Several index cards
Markers

Why Use This Strategy?
Intense interests can distract students with ASD from meaningful conversations. Without redirection, topics that students with ASD prefer can easily become the focus of speech. In addition, students with ASD can interject repetition of words or phrases from television or movies inappropriately throughout daily interactions.

The Out of the Box strategy helps students with ASD visualize a relationship between their speech and the topic of discussion. Further, this activity helps build attention to task.

How Does This Strategy Work?

- Ask the student with ASD an open-ended question. The question should be of high interest, but not a preferred topic. Sample open-ended questions follow.

- The child responds to the question, sharing as much information about the topic as he can. Encourage a detailed response by asking follow-up questions. (For example: "What else can you tell me about _____?")

- As the child shares, write each response on an index card. If the response fits the topic, place the card in the box. If the response is off topic, place the card outside the box.

- After the student has provided as much information as possible, remove the off-topic remarks. Then review the on-topic statements with the student.

Sample Questions

Tell me about . . .

- your brother or sister.
- a special toy.
- a friend.
- how you celebrate _____.
- how you get to school.

- your favorite vacation.
- your pet.
- your weekend.
- your favorite food.
- what you do after school.

Teacher Tips

- Keep in mind that offering relevant information to the conversation may be difficult for the student at first. Whenever possible help the student understand how on-topic statements are related to the discussion.

- For additional practice, allow the student to share his responses with a peer or another school adult. (For example: Ask the student to tell Miss Murray about his weekend.) Prompt the child to share details when necessary.

- As an extension to this activity, ask students to sort the information cards as on topic or off topic for each subject discussed.

Relevant IFSP or IEP Goals

Consider whether or not the following goals might be appropriate for children with ASD who are participating in the Out of the Box activity.

- Preschool—Student will engage in conversation initiated by others by providing relevant verbal responses.

- Kindergarten—Student will engage in conversation initiated by others by providing at least two relevant responses.

- First or second grade—Student will maintain conversation through at least three

exchanges by listening and responding appropriately to comments and questions.

Chatter Stations
Why Use This Strategy?

Scripting is common in some students with ASD. Like other perseverative behaviors, repetitive speech can help students with ASD ease anxiety or frustration. Therefore, it is often more beneficial to reduce or replace these behaviors rather than eliminate them entirely.

Chatter stations give students a place in the classroom to engage in scripting behavior. In this way, teachers can address the needs of students with ASD while also reducing class distractions.

How Does This Strategy Work?

- Select an area in the classroom to serve as the chatter station. The area should have a place to sit and very little decoration or other distractions.

- Self-advocacy is important for students with ASD. Work with the child to select a signal to use when he needs time to script during class. A card or hand signal works well, or the student can simply raise his hand to ask permission.

- Set a time limit for each visit to the chatter station. Use a timer to help students monitor their time and transition back to class.

Teacher Tips

- Carefully consider where the chatter station is placed. It is important that the chatter station does not look or feel like a punishment. A corner of a reading center provides a safe, quiet area.

- If you find that students are using the chatter station too often, use tokens to limit visits. When all tokens are used, the chatter station is available at teacher discretion only.

- Monitor the number of visits during the initial few days of use. Use that data to set a limit, and then reduce the number by two visits every three weeks.

Relevant IFSP or IEP Goals

Consider whether or not the following goals might be appropriate for children with ASD who are using Chatter Stations.

- Preschool—Student will reduce nonfunctional scripting behavior to no more than eight times per day for three consecutive weeks.

- Kindergarten—Student will reduce nonfunctional scripting behavior to no more than six times per day for four consecutive weeks.

- First or second grade—Student will reduce nonfunctional scripting behavior to no more than four times per day for six consecutive weeks.

Pocket Scripts
Why Use This Strategy?

Students with ASD must be taught social language. The more practice these students have with using social speech, the better they become at generalizing it to new situations.

Pocket scripts use scripting dialogue to help students with ASD interact with others appropriately in school. The small size of the pocket scripts provides individual support for the child with ASD in an unobtrusive way.

How Does This Strategy Work?

- Determine three to four social situations for which your students with ASD need to develop communication skills.

- Write a script that tells the student what words to use in specific social settings. See the sample pocket scripts that follow.

- Copy the scripts on cards small enough for students to carry in a pocket or in the palm of their hand. The small size makes the scripts easily accessible.

- Role-play with the student with ASD so he can practice using the pocket scripts appropriately.

Teacher Tips

- Consider adding pictures to the script text to help students visualize the social situation. This adaptation will also help prereaders use the pocket scripts.

- Use simple, child-friendly words and phrases in the pocket scripts so that the language sounds conversational.

- Sometimes the pocket scripts cannot be generalized to new situations. Teach your students with ASD how to deal with the frustration of being misunderstood.

- Laminate the pocket scripts to make them more durable. Attach cards with a metal binder ring. This makes it possible for you to easily replace mastered scripts with new ones.

- Teach typically developing peers to be compassionate toward their peers who are using pocket scripts. Encourage students to include and support their classmates.

Sample Pocket Scripts

Greeting Friends
I have many friends at school. When I see my friends at school, I will say, "Hi," and smile. If my friend asks me how I am, I will say, "I'm good today. How are you?"

Asking for Help
When I am at school, my teacher will give me work. If I feel confused or don't understand what to do, I will ask for help. First, I raise my hand. Then, I will say, "I need help. I don't understand." My teacher will help me. I will say "Thank you." Then, I will finish my work.

Borrowing an Eraser
We share many things at school. If I make a mistake, I can borrow an eraser from my friend. I will say, "Can I use your eraser?" If my friend says yes, I will take the eraser, use it, and then return it to my friend. I will tell my friend, "Thank you."

Playing with Friends
Sometimes we play at school. If I see my friends playing a game I want to play, I will say, "Can I play too?" If they say yes, I will sit down and play with my friends.

Relevant IFSP or IEP Goals
Consider whether or not the following goals might be appropriate for children with ASD who are using Pocket Scripts.

- Preschool—Given verbal or visual prompts, student will respond correctly to a question directed at him in three out of four opportunities.

- Kindergarten—Given verbal or visual prompts, the student will respond correctly to two questions asked consecutively of her in three out of four opportunities.

- First or second grade—With text models or cues, student will maintain a conversation across at least three exchanges two times during the school day.

The Guess What? Strategy
Why Use This Strategy?
Children with ASD can have problems naming common objects. Describing the characteristics of items is often even more difficult. Both of these skills are important because they help students generalize objects among many different groups of things.

In a game format, Guess What? helps students form questions about the attributes of classroom objects. Students also learn to think about objects based on size, shape, color, texture, and function.

How Does This Strategy Work?

- Select a common object from the classroom (such as an eraser, a pencil, a notepad, or a crayon) and place it in a paper bag.

- As a prompt, give an attribute category (size, color, shape, texture, or function). Have students ask yes-or-no questions within that category only. For instance, if the category is color, students would ask yes-or-no questions about the object's color. (For example: "Is it red? purple?")

- Once a yes response has been given, provide another category for students to offer questions.

- When a student has a guess, she should place her hand on the top of her head to signal to you that she has the answer.

- If the student guesses correctly, the game begins again with a new object. If the student guesses incorrectly, the current game continues.

Teacher Tips

- Use very basic objects during the first few times the game is played. Be sure that students have seen or used the object in class.

- This game is a fun way to introduce a lesson. For instance, a lesson on time might start with a Guess What? game using a watch or timer as the mystery item.

- Try using this game as a time-filler when an activity ends early or begins late.

- After several rounds of play, allow older children to select an object and lead the game.

Relevant IFSP or IEP Goals

Consider whether or not the following goals might be appropriate for children with ASD

who are participating in the Guess What? strategy.

- Preschool—Given a visual prompt, the student will provide an attribute about the object shown in four out of five opportunities.

- Kindergarten—Student will provide at least three attributes about an object with verbal prompting to describe color, shape, and size.

- First or second grade—Student will provide at least three attributes about an object without prompting.

The *Wh-* Sort Strategy
Materials
Felt sorting board (or 11" x 14" paper folded lengthwise into four equal rectangles)

Several (ten to fifteen) photographs or clip-art pictures of people, things, times, and places cut from old magazines, books, or printed computer images

Why Use This Strategy?
Answering and asking questions are significant components of the learning process. *Wh-* questions (*who?, what?, when?, where?,* and *why?*) reinforce verbal and visual understanding. Students with ASD sometimes struggle to respond to *wh-* questions because they have difficulty distinguishing among the question forms. This confusion can lead to misunderstanding and miscommunication.

The *wh-* sort activity helps students with ASD see patterns among the expected responses of *wh-* questions. This activity also provides visual support to answer each question type.

How Does This Strategy Work?

- At the top of each rectangle of the sorting board, write one of the following question words: *Who, What, When,* and *Where.*

- Explain that each question type has a unique question-response type. *Who* questions have people answers. *What* questions have thing answers. *When* questions have time answers (for example, day, night, summer, or spring). *Where* questions have place answers.

- Give each student pictures one at a time. Have the student sort the pictures on the sorting board under the appropriate question title. For instance, a picture of a tree would go under the *What* category, but a picture of a doctor would go under *Who*.

- When all of the pictures have been sorted, ask the student *wh-* questions about each picture. For example, "What plant has branches and leaves?" (a tree) or "Who helps you when you're sick?" (a doctor). Encourage the child to use the bank of photographs or pictures on the sorting board as support when necessary. Remove pictures from the sorting board as they are used.

Teacher Tips

- As a closing activity, include a few why questions. Help students understand that why questions explain.

- Once a picture set is mastered, replace five to seven mastered pictures with new ones.

- Include students in the process of picture selection to build their interest and sense of ownership of the activity. Allow them to choose pictures that represent favorite activities or objects. Ask families to provide photographs of special people or places.

- After several rounds of this activity, challenge students to answer the questions without the pictures by providing example answers in word form.

Relevant IFSP or IEP Goals

Consider whether or not the following goals might be appropriate for children with ASD who are participating in the *Wh-* Sort activity.

- Preschool—Given an array of three pictures of people, places, or objects, student will point to the picture that correctly answers a teacher-directed *wh-* question in eight out of ten opportunities.

- Kindergarten—Given an array of ten pictures of people, places, and objects, student will point to the picture that correctly answers a teacher-directed *wh-* question in eight out of ten opportunities.

- First or second grade—Student will answer teacher directed *wh-* questions correctly in eight out of ten opportunities.

The Three-Step Teacher Says Strategy
Why Use This Strategy?

Language development is about speaking and listening. Accordingly, teachers must help students learn to process information effectively.

Many young children, including students with ASD, need help developing these receptive language skills. Three-Step Teacher Says gives students an opportunity to practice listening and completing multistep tasks. This activity builds auditory memory skills as well.

How Does This Strategy Work?

- Give a series of three directions to the class or group (for example, "stand up, clap your hands, and touch your head").

- Monitor students as they complete each task. Students should complete each step in the order assigned.

- If students complete all three tasks correctly, they can earn tokens. When a child earns five tokens, you can give her a small reward or break time.

Teacher Tips

- Begin the activity by inserting short pauses between each direction. Shorten these pauses as students' skills improve.

- If three-step directions are too difficult, begin with two-step tasks. If students need a challenge, add a fourth step to the direction sequence.

- Pair responsible peers with students with ASD. Provide both students with opportunities to give and receive direction.

Relevant IFSP or IEP Goals

Consider whether or not the following goals might be appropriate for children with ASD who are participating in the Three-Step Teacher Says strategy.

- Preschool—Given oral instructions, the student will follow a simple one-step direction in four out of five opportunities.

- Kindergarten—Given oral instructions, the student will follow simple two-step directions in four out of five opportunities.

- First or second grade—Given oral instructions, the student will follow simple three-step directions in four out of five opportunities.

The Talking Tokens Strategy

Why Use This Strategy?

Maintaining a conversation can be difficult for students with ASD. Although higher-functioning students may want to interact with others, their focus is still on their own interests and thoughts. Consequently, conversations with students with ASD can feel very rigid and one-sided. This is especially true if a student has an obsession with one item or activity.

Talking Tokens limits students' comments on preferred topics. This activity will help students with ASD learn to maintain conversation by listening to others, asking questions, and taking turns.

How Does This Strategy Work?

- Determine one preferred conversation topic for your student with ASD.

- Explain why it is important to take turns in conversation and to talk about different topics (it keeps others interested in the conversation; it is polite to ask about others' interests).

- Give the student three tokens. Explain that these tokens must be "cashed in" to talk about the preferred interest. Each time the child discusses the topic, he must surrender one token. When all of the tokens are gone, the child cannot discuss that interest again unless the other person in the conversation discusses it.

- Begin a conversation with the student. Maintain the conversation through at least five exchanges, removing tokens as necessary.

Teacher Tips

- Adjust the number of tokens to the needs of the child. Children may need to begin with more tokens. Reduce the number of tokens as the student begins to feel more comfortable maintaining conversations.

- When the student's conversational skills improve, allow the child to practice with a peer. Monitor the conversation to ensure that both students are engaged.

- Teach the student ways he can transition the conversation to new topics (for example, by asking questions).

Relevant IFSP or IEP Goals

Consider whether or not the following goals might be appropriate for children with ASD who are participating in the Talking Tokens strategy.

- Preschool—When asked a question, the student will offer a relevant response in three out of five opportunities.

- Kindergarten—During a class discussion, the student will contribute at least one relevant comment each day for five consecutive days.

- First or second grade—Student will maintain a conversation across three exchanges, addressing at least one nonpreferred topic.

Technology Supports to Build Speech and Language Skills

- Visit Speaking of Speech (http://www.speakingofspeech.com/Materials_Exchange.php) to take advantage of free speech-and-language materials and a resource exchange.

- Use interactive board games, such as those available for free at Speech-Language Resources (http://www.speechlanguage-resources.com/free-board-games.html), to teach practical language skills. Other free classroom materials are also available on this website.

- Start a conversation with your students with small-talk questions for children featured at Positive Parenting Connection (http://www.positiveparentingconnection.net/40-questions-that-get-kids-talking/). Questions focus on a variety of child-friendly interests.

- Speech and Language Kids (http://www.speechandlanguagekids.com/) has an abundance of free speech and language content organized by topic and age, including information, activities, and resources.

- Review strategies for supporting students with ASD, including this post about dealing with topic perseveration at Autism Classroom Resources (http://www.autismclassroomresources.com/truing-to-pull-out-of-perseveration/), a blog written by ASD consultant Christine Reeve.

- Use the following-direction activities at Making Learning Fun (http://www.makinglearningfun.com/themepages/FollowingDirectionsDirectory.html) to build receptive language.

- Use crafts to reinforce attention to directions. DLTK's Crafts for Kids (http://www.dltk-kids.com/) has numerous thematic crafts to infuse classroom learning with the arts.

- Autism Speaks (http://www.autismspeaks.org/autism-apps) has compiled a list of several mobile apps to help strengthen skills in individuals with ASD. Many of these apps support speech and language development.

- Create your own picture symbols for daily class activities or common phrases at Do2Learn (http://do2learn.com/picturecards/printcards/).

- Use sign language to include students with ASD. Find an American Sign Language video dictionary for common words at Handspeak (http://www.handspeak.com/word/).

- Signing Time (http://www.signingtime.com/resources/activities) has an assortment of videos, games, and activities that incorporate sign language.

Key Terms

- **articulation:** The production of sounds in speech.

- **augmentative and alternative communication (AAC):** Other than speech, all methods of communication, including gestures, written text, or use of simple or complex tools.

- **communication:** The use of speech text or gestures to exchange information.

- **echolalia:** The repetition of a word or phrase after it is said.

- **expressive communication:** The use of words to communicate.

- **fluency:** The smoothness and pace of speech.
- **functional communication:** Communication which holds shared meaning for both the speaker and the receiver.
- **language:** How speech is spoken, processed, and understood.

- **nonfunctional communication:** Communication which holds meaning for the speaker alone.
- **receptive communication:** Processing and understanding language.
- **scripting:** Delayed repetition of a word or phrase, often from television or movies.

4 Teaching Learners with ASD to Read and Write

It is sustained silent reading (SSR) time in Ms. Kline's first-grade classroom. As the teacher walks around the classroom, she sees many of her students are quietly reading books to themselves. However, one first grader is definitely not reading. Cooper loves trains, and he has taken advantage of this less-structured class time to play with toy trains from his backpack. Ms. Kline removes the trains from his desk and replaces them with a book about a cat. She explains to Cooper that this book is at his just-right reading level. He opens the first page and reads a few of the sight words. Although Cooper knows his letters and many letter sounds, he becomes frustrated when the teacher tries to help him sound out unfamiliar words from the book. Cooper rips pages from the cat book, throws it on the floor, and grabs the toy trains from the teacher's desk. At the end of SSR time, Ms. Kline asks students to write about what they have read. Cooper begins to draw a train on his paper. When his teacher corrects him, he writes a list of words on the paper. His writing is difficult to read because the words are in no clear order and many letters are not properly formed or positioned on the paper (for example, upside down or reversed). When Ms. Kline asks Cooper to share his work with the class, he crumples up his paper and hides under his desk. Ms. Kline feels pressured by all of the talk of meeting standards and how her students' scores will be used to evaluate her performance as a teacher.

The Significance of Literacy

Particularly for the early childhood classroom, learning to read and write is a top priority. The acquisition of basic literacy skills supports learning in all areas and facilitates independence. With the ability to read and write, students can receive and process information, and they can also use resources to answer questions and extend their thinking. Additionally, reading and writing skills help students connect with others through common knowledge and experiences. In these ways, literacy prepares students to contribute and function within their communities.

For students with ASD, literacy skills have an even greater importance. Communication challenges are a common characteristic of ASD. Delays in language and speech disorders are common. Frequent reading and writing practice not only improves language development but also has a ripple effect on other developmental areas. For example, the ability to decipher print offers students with ASD language models that, with guidance, can be transferred to speech. This speech might then be used as a "script" to guide conversation with a peer. Further, strong reading and writing skills can offer students with ASD an alternative means to express themselves. In fact, many assistive communication tools and devices incorporate reading or writing skills.

However, as Cooper's story illustrates, teaching students with ASD to be good readers and writers can present various challenges to teachers. What might Cooper's teacher have done differently? First of all, Ms. Kline could have built on his interests. Because Cooper is clearly fascinated with trains, the teacher could have used this preference to motivate him to complete assigned reading and writing activities. Consider how Cooper's attention might have increased if Ms. Kline had offered him a book about trains to read or suggested that he draw train tracks with some words on them and then drive the train around on the page. Capitalizing on Cooper's interests could motivate him to learn unfamiliar words as well as build greater interest in writing.

Students with ASD rarely follow a typical development pattern. Instead, their skill growth is often irregular, making students with ASD proficient in some areas, but lacking in others. For instance, a child with ASD may be able to read words fluently, but have little comprehension of the text. This phenomenon may be particularly evident when the text focuses on a character's feelings or motives. For instance, a five-year-old on the autism spectrum could read the text of *Goldilocks and the Three Bears* but could not explain what Goldilocks meant when she said the porridge was "just right." Such gaps in students' skills along with their possibly limited interests can make traditional methods of instruction ineffective. Students with ASD often need direct instruction in reading and writing skills, including step-by-step guidance on how to plan and organize tasks. At its very essence, literacy relies on information processing, and to improve their reading and writing skills, many students with ASD simply must learn to think differently.

The Role of Executive Function on Literacy Development

Poor executive-function skills can explain differences in thinking patterns for many students with ASD. As Christina Carnahan and her coauthors explained in their journal article, executive functioning describes how the brain sorts, categorizes, and arranges information. Executive-function skills are very different from simply knowing about an assignment or activity; students use these skills to plan how to complete a task. A student with ASD may understand that writing a story means producing sentences in a logical order. However, this same student may struggle with how to create that story. Research by Sally Ozonoff and David Strayer suggests that executive functioning influences thinking flexibility, working memory, goal planning, and self-monitoring.

Thinking Flexibility

Flexible thinkers consider multiple ways to begin and complete a task. Thinking with flexibility allows students to shift the way they approach an activity and to adapt to changes in expectations. Reading and writing requires well-developed thinking flexibility. While reading and writing, students must be able to think about many parts of a text at once and to make decisions about their understanding. When interpreting a single story, there are many different aspects that need to be orchestrated in order to achieve understanding. At various times during reading, students are expected to identify the plot, characters, main idea, and supporting details.

Working Memory

Working memory might be conceptualized as the mental workspace of the brain. One simple way to think of working memory is to imagine that it is a whiteboard with a limited amount of space to hold the material that the brain is working on at any given time. Working memory is tied to executive function because, without ideas held in memory, learners do not have access to the resources that they need to think through a task. Suppose, for example, that a child is performing an everyday task such as preparing a breakfast of cereal and milk. Think about all of the things that must be easily accessed in the brain—the location of the cereal, milk, bowls, and spoons; how to pour from the cereal box and milk carton; and so on. It is noteworthy that this task is intrinsically motivating because the child gets a bowl of cereal to eat at the end of the sequence.

Literacy tasks are more abstract and less intrinsically motivating, and this makes them more difficult. This is especially difficult in reading and writing because the steps for these skills are often less defined than common daily tasks. To write a sentence, students must begin the first word with a capital letter, place letters and words in logical order, and complete the sentence with proper punctuation. A limited working memory makes recall of even repeated procedures difficult.

Goal Planning

Even when children with ASD understand how to complete a task, they still must be able to follow steps logically to meet a goal. This is why goal planning is so important. In a typical early childhood classroom, students are taught how to follow steps to finish an assignment. Consider the way goal planning affects a common reading task:

- The teacher sets a goal: Students must read a book for sustained silent reading (SSR).

- The student processes the goal and identifies the steps necessary to accomplish the goal. The child has to go to the reading center, select a book, return to her desk, and begin reading.

- The student must be self-directed to stay focused on the goal. Although the child sees others playing computer games on the way to the reading center, she must concentrate on selecting and reading a book.

Through experience and practice, most school-age children learn how to adjust their goal planning when circumstances change (when the child must read a book selected for her) or when they need to transfer skills to new activities (when the child must partner-read). In contrast, many students with ASD struggle to break predictable patterns of behavior and to ignore distractions. Because writing and reading tasks tend to vary in topic and emphasis, deficits in goal planning can have a profound effect on student progress in these areas.

Self-Monitoring

Metacognition is often defined as the ability to think about one's own thinking. For example, a child who is reading may realize that, because he does not know the meaning of an important word, he has lost comprehension. His solutions might include such strategies as asking a peer or the teacher, reading to the end of the sentence to see if he can figure out the word, studying the illustrations for clues, and so on. Self-monitoring is a student's ability to think about his thinking as it is happening. Students who self-monitor engage in reflective practices to correct errors and to adjust to changes within individual tasks. Well-developed self-monitoring skills allow children to use effective strategies to meet the objectives within assignments.

See table 4.1 for some examples of these strategies, which can help students split attention among multiple parts of a task. For example, during a class read-aloud, a student should be engaged in a number of tasks including, but not limited to, listening to the text read aloud, monitoring the story in pictures, identifying the main idea and story details, and interpreting characters' feelings.

Developing Executive-Function Skills

Teachers can use some of the strategies shown in table 4.1 to help children develop more skill in particular areas of executive function.

Adapting Literacy Assignments

Consider the elements of executive functioning: thinking flexibility, working memory, goal planning, and self-monitoring. Use the following organizer to plan how to adapt a literacy assignment to strengthen these skills in students with ASD.

Table 4.1 Classroom Strategies for Improving Skill in Areas of Executive Function

Thinking Flexibility	Working Memory	Goal Planning	Self-Monitoring
With warning, make minor changes to students' schedules. Teach specific coping strategies to deal with these changes.	Use memory card games to reinforce learning of rote skills (for example, sight words, spelling patterns, and vocabulary).	Encourage students to visualize themselves completing each step of a task before beginning an assignment. When necessary, use picture cues as support.	Require students to stop at multiple points in a reading to summarize the text. Teach students how to reread text to correct errors.
Incorporate daily word studies of language with multiple meanings (for example, *stamp, check,* and *bark*). Assist students in exploring common grade-appropriate idioms (for example, *take it easy, quiet as a mouse*).	Pair the introduction of new information with interactive, engaging tasks. Students will be more likely to recall new information that has been linked to novel tasks.	Allow students to recite or write the steps of a task before completing it. Draw attention to errors and assist students in self-correction.	Irene O'Connor and Perry Klein explain a technique called anaphoric cueing, which teaches students to pay close attention to pronoun referents as they read. This strategy helps students keep track of the who and what of a narrative.
Offer assignment options to students. Encourage students to use art, drama, poetry, or music to express understanding of a topic.	Model the use of songs, rhymes, or mnemonic devices to remember important facts or information. Encourage students to work with partners to create their own devices.	Make use of graphic organizers or checklists to help students organize the steps and order of a task or assignment.	Teach students to track print with their fingers and read aloud their written work. These strategies help students hear and see errors in their work.

Assignment Planning Template

Subject:
Topic:
Grade Level:
Materials:

Thinking Flexibility: How will students think about lesson ideas in new or different ways?

Working Memory: How will students remember the steps in completing the lesson activities?

Goal Planning: How will students be supported in completing the lesson activities?

Self-Monitoring: How will students reflect on their learning during the lesson?

Challenges with Reading Comprehension

Weaknesses in executive functioning help explain why reading comprehension frequently poses a struggle for students with ASD. Because many of these students have limited flexibility in their thinking, it is difficult to use prior knowledge and experience to create meaning from a text. Limitations in memory and goal planning make it challenging for students to recall and use strategies to help them comprehend text. Further, intense interests in specific topics can distract students as they read, making it almost impossible to self-monitor their understanding.

A concept known as theory of mind also adds to challenges of comprehension of fictional works. Researchers Ifat Gamliel and Nurit Yirmiya explain that theory of mind suggests that students with ASD struggle to interpret the perspective and feelings of others. Certainly, this type of deficit can influence how students interact with others, but it also can undermine comprehension of text. Comprehension not only refers to understanding what is read, but also describing, predicting, and inferring the thoughts and behaviors of characters. Because students with ASD cannot always recognize the feelings and perspectives of others, these complex reading skills can be difficult for them to grasp.

Ideas for Improving Listening and Reading Comprehension in Students with ASD
Before Listening or Reading

● Take a picture walk through the book to build prior knowledge. Use not only fictional storybooks but also factual information books. Help students make predictions about what will happen in the story or what they think they might learn. Write their predictions and put their names or initials next to each one. Give them a chance to revise predictions as the story progresses.

● Tap into students' prior knowledge with a K-W-L-S chart in which they fill out the first two columns prior to reading the text (*What We Know* and *What We Want to Know*) and fill out the last two columns after hearing or reading (*What We Learned* and *What We Still Want to Know*). Help students make connections between their interests and the text.

- Present any vocabulary that might be unfamiliar or difficult for students to understand. Use images as well as words.

During Listening or Reading

- Set listeners' expectations by telling them what to listen for (for example, repetition of a special word or rhyming pairs). Whenever possible, encourage students to read aloud with an adult volunteer, cross-age tutor, or peer. This helps students correct their errors on the spot and limits internal distractions while reading.

- Ask students questions about what is happening in the story. Review passages that students seem to misunderstand. Recap the text periodically to facilitate comprehension.

- Remember that students with ASD are often visual learners, so consider using story structure organizers to help students summarize the text as they read.

After Listening or Reading

- Revisit the text verbally and teach students to reread text to locate information. Use highlighter tape or highlighter markers to draw attention to details in stories or articles.

- Encourage students to draw pictures to describe the plot of a story or to explain the details of a nonfiction text.

- Complete and review graphic organizers that correspond to the type of text. Add details from the text as necessary.

Writing Skills Deficit

There are a number of reasons why writing is so difficult for students with ASD. Similar to reading, writing involves the orchestration of several skills at once. According to a study by Cheryl Boucher and Kathy Oehler, language, organization, motor control and planning, and sensory processing play equally important roles in writing development. When deficits exist in one or more of these areas, writing poses a special challenge to students with ASD. This is why it is so important that teachers consider the ways ASD can affect writing and intervene with useful practices in the classroom.

Skills that can influence writing development and affect classroom tasks include the following:

Oral Language and Composition

- Coordinating ideas with topics
- Organizing thoughts into sentences
- Interpreting the purpose of an assignment or activity

Organization

- Formatting ideas into written text
- Using correct word order in words and sentences

Motor Control and Planning

- Positioning the paper
- Holding the writing tool
- Aligning the text to the paper
- Forming letters

Sensory Processing

- Focusing on writing or listening tasks
- Blocking out external visual or auditory stimuli

Oral Language and Composition

Speech and writing are related. Many beginning writers write in a way that imitates how they speak. Deficits in how language is understood and processed, however, make the writing process significantly more difficult for students with ASD. Although students with ASD may have knowledge or interest in a particular subject, writing about the topic can be challenging because of language barriers. Coordinating relevant ideas with a selected topic, organizing thoughts into sentences, or simply interpreting the purpose of the writing assignment all depend on the student's ability to understand language. The following are suggestions for overcoming language challenges in writing for students with ASD:

- Accept all efforts at writing; for example, a linear scribble can be used to imitate what adults appear to be doing when they are quickly writing something in cursive handwriting.

- Convey the message that the marks themselves mean something with comments such as, "It says . . ." or "Look, we have a message . . ." or "Someone sent us a letter in the mail . . . ."

- Have an aide or volunteer write captions for the child's drawings or take dictation.

- Take the time to explain writing assignments thoroughly. Provide examples and be sure students understand the purpose for writing and the assignment expectations.

- Encourage students to engage in pre-writing activities. For example, students may be able to begin writing assignments more easily if they are given an opportunity to play with a toy farm set before listening to a story, talking, or drawing about farms.

- Make use of writing routines to give students frequent practice with specific writing assignments. Provide multiple occasions for students to write about similar topics or ideas. For instance, the narrative writing assignment on Mondays could be to write about students' weekend activities.

Organization

Once students with ASD understand a writing task, they still must be able to organize their thoughts into text. However, many young students with ASD have difficulty planning their writing ideas. Even ordering simple sentences

requires complex organization. To write text that is understandable to others, students must have an idea, format the idea as a sentence, and produce the sentence on paper. For many students with ASD, following these steps in logical order is tremendously challenging. To improve students' writing organization, teachers can consider these ideas for working with individual children or as part of a large-group assignment:

- Show students how to use graphic organizers to plan their ideas before writing. Help students transfer their ideas from the organizer to paper.

- Whenever possible, allow students to write a draft of their writing. Use colored pens and markers to write notes on students' drafts explaining how to improve the writing sequence.

- Use manipulatives to allow students to "see" how sentences or paragraphs are built. Write one word or one sentence on each item (for example, a block, card, or sticky note) and help students move the words or sentences to form logical sentences or paragraphs.

Motor Control and Planning

For many young students, the physical aspect of writing itself can be troublesome. Although students with ASD may be able to identify letters correctly, their brains may have difficulty sending messages to their bodies to produce these letters on the page. As a result, a task as simple as tracing letters can be very overwhelming for children with ASD. These are some ways teachers can support students with motor control and planning:

- Create routines that invite children to communicate through drawing and writing, such as having a mailbox for each child, having a classroom helper deliver the mail, or sending get-well-soon and thank-you cards to classmates and visitors.

- Take children on a walking tour of the center or school. Give them clipboards and pencils, and have them draw or write lists of places where they see people writing.

- Allow students to practice producing letters through tactile experiences. Students can trace with their fingers letters cut from felt or foam.

- Invest in pencil grippers or pencil weights. Both of these tools help students receive sensory input as they write while also helping with coordination.

- Permit students to dictate their writing to a teacher or peer. Allow students to trace the writing with either a pencil or a finger.

- Equip play areas with writing materials; for example, a prescription pad, a calendar, and a cash register at a pretend veterinary office.

Sensory Processing

In a typical school, there is a tremendous amount of sensory stimulation and children can be overwhelmed by the environment. A well-equipped preschool, for example, often has large windows, bright colors, inviting toys, and interesting displays. While many children are able to ignore common classroom sights and sounds, visual and auditory input can be an ongoing distraction for students with ASD. To focus on a task, including one as complex as writing, students with ASD must learn to block outside sensory stimuli. Although it can be difficult to anticipate what sights, sounds, or smells will be taxing for an individual student, there are some ways that teachers can limit sensory overload:

- Place small boards on students' desks to create privacy and limit nearby distractions as they write.

- Allow students to wear headphones while writing to muffle outside sounds.

- Give students seating options while writing (children can stand, straddle the chair, sit on knees, and so on) and allow students to change positions as necessary. This type of movement allows students to manage sensory input.

Writer's Blocks

Read each scenario. Which skill—language, organization, motor planning and control, or sensory processing—needs additional support to improve the student's writing development?

1. Casey dictates a creative story about his family's dog, but has difficulty transferring the story to paper.

2. Reggie cannot focus on writing a sentence about his weekend because his chair feels too hard.

3. When asked to draw and write the name of a friend, Joanna writes a telephone number from a commercial she saw last night.

4. Mr. Benson asks students to write a sentence about their favorite season. Kenny writes a list of words: football, leaves, jumping.

Answers
1. motor planning and control; 2. sensory processing; 3. language; and 4. organization.

Motivating Students with ASD to Read and Write

With support and guidance, students with ASD can develop functional reading and writing skills. Although literacy may be at the heart of many early childhood classrooms, simply repeating skills will not build motivation to read and write. Encouraging students with ASD who struggle with these skills is often even more difficult. The following suggestions are ways to promote motivation to read and write in young students with ASD:

- **Tap into individual interests.** Students with ASD often have very intense interests. Tailor assignments to give students frequent opportunities to read and write about these interests.

- **Incorporate technology.** Technology can make listening, reading, and writing assignments more interactive and engaging. Give students opportunities to speak and have their words recorded; to listen to and watch stories that have the text scripted or highlighted as each word is spoken; or if they are more advanced, to illustrate and type original stories using computer software.

- **Match assignment tasks with individual students' needs.** Set students with ASD up for success by adapting assignments to meet their needs. Chunk larger assignments into smaller, more manageable parts so that tasks are less daunting.

- **Teach students to self-select appropriate books.** Young children, especially, rely on book covers to choose what to read. Encourage students to select books that they can read independently, even if these books have limited text or have only pictures.

- **Expose students to a variety of books and writing types.** Young children may not be aware of the many different types of text available to them. Integrate different types of writing, such as poetry, narrative, nonfiction, and advertisements, into daily activities. Include a wide selection of books in the classroom library.

- **Encourage students to write or tell for a real audience.** Students will tell or write with a purpose when they speak or write with a specific audience in mind. Encourage students with ASD to share with classmates, younger peers, or special adults within the school community.

- **Celebrate successes.** Keep in mind that reading and writing are skills that improve with frequent feedback on progress. Offer supportive guidance, but praise students for their effort and achievements.

Literacy skills are the foundation for subsequent learning experiences. Through reading and writing, students learn to process information, problem-solve, and communicate their thoughts and ideas. For students with ASD, acquiring these skills requires more direct instruction. The following strategies suggest ways to teach students with ASD to improve their literacy skills.

Strategies to Help Students with ASD Become Better Readers and Writers

The Handwriting Dance Strategy
Why Use This Strategy?

Handwriting skills can develop more slowly for some students with ASD. Poor motor planning makes letter and number formation extremely challenging, even for students with high-functioning ASD. Because writing is such an integral part of classroom learning, it is easy to see why good printing skills benefit students with ASD in inclusive classrooms.

The handwriting dance strategy uses large movement to teach letter and number formation. Using their bodies, students practice letter shapes and patterns, creating muscle memory and aiding the transfer of skills to paper.

How Does This Strategy Work?

- Select a single letter or number to practice with students. Review the formation steps for the selected letter or number.

- Using large, exaggerated movements make the selected letter or number in the air with your hand.

- Encourage students to practice making the letter or number with you, using similar movements.

- Once students appear comfortable with large movements, transition to smaller more precise movements. For example, students can make the letter with a finger or an elbow.

- Give students an opportunity to trace the movements on paper with their fingers or a writing tool. Offer feedback on letter or number formation as needed.

Teacher Tips

- When modeling letter or number movements, be sure to mirror your movements so that the formation is correct from the students' point-of-view.

- Tap into students' creativity in this assignment. Have the class pretend that they are painting letters on an imaginary large canvas, using their hands as extra-large paintbrushes.

- Play soft, soothing music while practicing letter and number movements. Make the movements faster or slower in response to changes in the music's tempo.

Relevant IFSP or IEP Goals

Consider whether or not the following goals might be appropriate for children with ASD

who are participating in the Handwriting Dance strategy.

- Preschool—Student will write the uppercase and lowercase letters in her first name with correct formation and spacing in three out of four opportunities.

- Kindergarten—Student will write the uppercase and lowercase letters in her first and last name with correct formation and spacing in three out of four opportunities.

- First or second grade—From a teacher model, the student will copy a complete sentence with correct formation and spacing in three out of four opportunities.

Yellow-Line Writing
Materials
Writing paper with lines
Yellow marker
Pencil

Why Use This Strategy?
Dictation can be an effective way for students with poor handwriting to participate in writing activities. Because of irregular development of skills, it is not unusual for some students with ASD to be able to express ideas verbally, but struggle to put them in print.

Yellow-line writing gives students with this particular skillset an opportunity to see their ideas on paper while practicing correct letter formation and spacing. This strategy offers students real ownership of their ideas while also providing legible content for an audience.

How Does This Strategy Work?

- Select a writing topic or sentence starter. Brainstorm appropriate responses with individual students or with the class.

- Ask the student to share her response to the writing topic or sentence starter.

- Using a yellow marker, write the child's response with proper letter formation and spacing.

- Have the student trace over the yellow writing with a pencil.

Teacher Tips

- Remember that yellow-line writing acts as a model for students. Be sure to print neatly and with recommended formation.

- For students who need less support, write only a portion of the writing assignment. Make students accountable for writing at least some portion of the task independently.

- Yellow-line writing can be used to assist students who need support spelling unfamiliar words. Use this technique to help students incorporate new words in their writing.

Relevant IFSP or IEP Goals

Consider whether or not the following goals might be appropriate for children with ASD who are using the Yellow-Line Writing strategy.

- Preschool—When given a topic, the student will verbally state a relevant one-word response to the topic independently in four out of five opportunities.

- Kindergarten—Student will trace with a pencil at least three words with proper letter formation and spacing.

- First or second grade—Student will trace with a pencil at least one complete sentence with proper letter formation and spacing.

The Writing Tokens Strategy
Materials
Small manipulatives
Writing paper

Why Use This Strategy?
Writing is a complex skill. It involves thinking about ideas, organizing thoughts, and producing text logically. Because students with ASD struggle with communication, the process of writing can be difficult for these learners.

The writing tokens strategy can help young children plan their writing. Using visual manipulatives, this strategy allows beginning writers to organize their ideas before transferring them to paper.

How Does This Strategy Work?

- Suggest a writing topic or story starter for students.

- As a class, brainstorm possible responses to the selected writing prompt.

- Have students speak their responses to the writing prompt one at a time. Have students line up one token for each word in their sentence. For example, the sentence *I have a red apple* has five words, so there would be five tokens in a row.

- Students should touch each token as they say the words in their oral responses. Repeat this step as needed to help students understand the sentence sequence.

- Have students move their tokens to writing paper. Again, students should say the words in their sentences as they place each token in a line above the writing space on the paper.

- Ask students to transfer their ideas to paper by writing one word of the sentence at a time. When the sentence is complete, have students check their writing by matching each token to its corresponding word in the sentence.

- Repeat the process with additional sentences as needed.

Teacher Tips

- Keep in mind that students with ASD may need help organizing their thoughts or sequencing words. Provide prompts as necessary.

- For students who struggle with spelling, write unfamiliar words on small sticky notes and place them in the appropriate space on the writing paper.

- Incorporate the yellow-line writing strategy with this technique to support students who have difficulty with letter formation.

- For younger students who are not yet writing, implement this strategy as a whole-group activity or use it to help students organize their oral responses.

Relevant IFSP or IEP Goals

Consider whether or not the following goals might be appropriate for children with ASD who are using the Writing Tokens strategy.

- Preschool—When given a topic, the student will verbally state a relevant one-word response to the topic independently in four out of five opportunities.

- Kindergarten—When given a topic, the student will dictate a relevant response to the topic in four out of five opportunities.

- First or second grade—When given a topic, the student will write at least one complete sentence independently in four out of five opportunities.

Draw the Story: A One-to-One Strategy
Materials
Book or narrative
Writing paper
Pencils

Why Use This Strategy?
A combination of poor self-monitoring skills and an inability to see multiple perspectives makes reading comprehension challenging for many students with ASD. These deficits cause students to struggle with predicting and interpreting text.

The Draw the Story strategy is based on the idea that many people create visual images in their minds as they read. Many students with ASD are visual learners. The Draw the Story strategy uses this strength to build reading comprehension. By using focus questions about the story structure, students with ASD can draw their understanding of stories.

How Does This Strategy Work?

- Select a narrative text for the student to read. Be sure that the text matches the reading readiness level for the child and has a strong story structure (characters, setting, and plot).

- Develop a list of focus questions about the story structure. Some suggested focus questions follow.

- Write each question at the top of a piece of paper. Preview the list of focus questions with the student.

- Have the student begin reading the text. As the student arrives at places within the text that answer one or more of the focus questions, prompt her to respond to the question verbally and then draw a response

- When the student has read the entire text and answered each focus question, review

Suggested Focus Questions

- *Who is this story about?*
- *Where does this story take place?*
- *What happens first, next, and last?*
- *What is the problem in this story?*
- *How is the problem solved?*
- *How does this story end?*

both her visual and verbal responses. Assist the student in summarizing what she read.

Teacher Tips

- When selecting practice texts, remember that the fluency of a child with ASD may be stronger than his comprehension skills. It may be necessary to select books slightly below a child's reading level in order to meet his comprehension needs.

- Select books that are high-interest for the student with ASD.

- When using nonfiction selections, it is important to develop questions that are directly linked to concepts and ideas present in the book.

- Encourage the student to use his visual summary to retell the story to another teacher or a peer.

Relevant IFSP or IEP Goals

Consider whether or not the following goals might be appropriate for children with ASD who are using the Draw the Story strategy.

- Preschool—After a story is read aloud to the class, the student will name correctly the main character from the story in four out of five opportunities with visual prompting.

- Kindergarten—After a story is read aloud to the class, the student will name correctly at least one event from the story in four out of five opportunities with visual prompting.

- First or second grade—After reading a developmentally-appropriate narrative text, the student will retell the story using at least three key details about the story structure (characters, setting, and plot) in three out of four opportunities.

Reading Running Start: A Partner Reading Strategy
Materials
Reading material

Why Use This Strategy?
Listening to students read aloud is one way that teachers can monitor student fluency. However, it can be difficult to keep some students with ASD engaged in reading, especially when the text holds limited personal meaning.

Giving students with ASD a reading running start helps them begin reading a passage aloud with proper rate and expression. Further, this strategy encourages students to maintain focus and to track print text as it is read aloud.

How Does This Strategy Work?

- Select an age-appropriate passage that matches the readiness level of the student.

- Preview the reading passage with the student. Incorporate appropriate strategies to tap into the student's prior knowledge or to establish text-to-student connections.

- Begin reading the first few words of the passage, and then stop. Have the student take over and continue to read from the place where you stopped.

- At various points in the read-aloud, join in reading with the student to model proper reading rate, word accuracy, or expression. You may also provide the student with another reading running start if he becomes distracted or disengaged while reading.

Teacher Tips

- When possible, both you and the student should have your own copies of the reading passage. Model using a finger to track print while reading. Encourage the student to do the same.

- Reading running starts do not need to begin with the first word of a sentence and end at the ending punctuation. After the initial running start, begin and end running starts at various points in the text. This motivates students with ASD to follow along in the passage as the teacher reads.

- For shorter passages, direct the student to reread the text without a running start.

- After the student reads the passage, ask him questions about the text. Summarize or organize the content of the text with a graphic organizer.

Relevant IFSP or IEP Goals

Consider whether or not the following goals might be appropriate for children with ASD who are using the Reading Running Start strategy.

- Preschool—From a baseline score of _____, student will improve his recognition of capital and lowercase letters by at least ten letters.

- Kindergarten—From a baseline score of _____, student will improve his recognition of Dolch sight words by at least ten words.

- First or second grade—From a baseline score of _____, student will improve reading fluency to _____ as measured by running records, DIBELS, reading fluency benchmarks, and so on.

Sound Charades

Materials

Index cards
Marker

Why Use This Strategy?

Phonics is critical to the development of literacy skills. Pairing letter formation with corresponding sounds helps students recognize the sound parts of words. Being able to recognize these letter and sound patterns in words helps students read unfamiliar words.

Sound charades uses letter cards to reinforce letter sounds and patterns. Because students with ASD are often visual learners, this strategy allows students to improve decoding skills. Sound charades also incorporates both sound and movement, which can help sensory learners retain new information.

How Does This Strategy Work?

- Select a set of single letters (such as *a, m,* and *n*), consonant digraphs (such as *sh, th,* and *ng*), or vowel digraphs (such as *ea, ay,* and *oo*). Create cards with the letters printed in the center.

- Model the sound associated with the letters on each card.

- Work with students to create movement patterns for each letter set. Develop a list of words that begin with each letter sound. Model ways to pantomime words that begin with the letter or letter sound. See the suggested movements for example sound cards that follow. Practice the sounds and movements of the card set. Once children recognize several sounds and motions, they can act out short words by combining sounds and motions (for example, for /c/, /ă/, and /b/: cutting, moving finger in tsk-tsk motion, bouncing a ball).

Example Movements for Sound Charades
Consonants and consonant digraphs:

/c/ pantomime cutting

/b/ move hand up and down as if bouncing a ball

/h/ panting as if out of breath

/v/ pantomime starting a motorcycle

/ph/ picking up the phone

/ch/ move arms like a chugging train

Vowels and vowel digraphs:

/ă/ move finger in a tsk-tsk motion while shaking head no

/ĕ/ make a long elephant trunk

/ŭ/ point up

/ī/ point to oneself

/ey/ move arms like a monkey

/oa/ pantomime putting on a coat

Teacher Tips

● Include students in the process of choosing motions for each sound card. In this way, students have ownership in the game, which builds student participation and interest.

● Incorporate some sign language signs into the game. This provides additional support for students with communication needs.

● Encourage students to lead the game as they become more familiar with it. Have students select words that use the sound patterns of the sound cards they know.

Relevant IFSP or IEP Goals

Consider whether or not the following goals might be appropriate for children with ASD who are using the Sound Charades strategy.

● Preschool—Student will demonstrate an understanding of letter/sound relationships by correctly recognizing consonant sound cards independently.

● Kindergarten—Student will demonstrate an understanding of letter/sound relationships by correctly recognizing consonant and vowel sound cards independently.

● First or second grade—Student will demonstrate an understanding of letter/ sound relationships by combining sound cards to build words independently.

Literacy Graphic Organizers

Materials
Printouts of graphic organizers

Why Use This Strategy?
From the perspective of many students with ASD, school delivers an enormous amount of abstract information. It can be difficult for these learners to make sense of information that appears disconnected and unimportant.

Graphic organizers help students with ASD manage large amounts of information. By classifying information so that it is easier to access and understand, graphic organizers help students build comprehension, visualize relationships among topics, and categorize ideas and thoughts.

How Does This Strategy Work?

● Graphic organizers are practical and useful tools. There are many available that support literacy work in early childhood classrooms. The first step in using literacy graphic organizers is to find one that fits the reading or writing assignment. You can find graphic organizers suitable for early childhood students in the list of websites in the Technology Resources section of this chapter.

● Select a graphic organizer that is appropriate for the lesson or activity. Because there are many different types of graphic organizers, it is important to become familiar with the format and guidelines of the organizer before using it in class.

● Provide students with guided practice using the graphic organizer.

● Support students in using the graphic organizer independently.

Teacher Tips

● Model using graphic organizers in the whole-class setting. Show students how to use graphic organizers to brainstorm, plan, and complete assignments.

- Introduce graphic organizers through high-interest writing assignments or book selections. Show students how the process can be fun.

- Allow students to partner to complete graphic organizers. Be available to offer students support and guidance.

- Encourage students to explain their completed graphic organizers. Ask students to make connections between ideas.

Relevant IFSP or IEP Goals

Consider whether or not the following goals might be appropriate for children with ASD who are using Literacy Graphic Organizers.

- Preschool—Given a graphic organizer completed in a whole-group setting, the student will name correctly at least two characters from the story in four out of five opportunities from a narrative text read aloud to her.

- Kindergarten—Given a graphic organizer, the student will draw the setting, characters, and plot of a narrative text read aloud to him.

- First or second grade—Given a graphic organizer, student will use words and pictures to identify the setting, characters, and plot of a narrative text read aloud to her.

Technology Resources to Support Literacy Skills in Students with ASD

- Teach students to be flexible thinkers by challenging them with the child-friendly jokes and riddles at Kid Jokes of the Day (http://www.kidsjokesoftheday.com/).

- Visit Starfall (http://www.starfall.com/) for a variety of online literacy games and activities

for early childhood students at various reading levels.

- Children will love ABCya (http://www.abcya.com/), which features tons of educational games and apps organized by grade level.

- Use popular characters to teach basic literacy skills at PBS Kids (http://pbskids.org/). The site includes several educational-based videos as well as fun games, activities, printables.

- Encourage your students to write by allowing them to design their own writing paper. DLTK's Crafts for Kids (http://www.dltk-cards.com/writingpaper/cpaper1.asp) provides several different options for themes and line spacing.

- Practice handwriting formation and spacing with Kidzone's tracer pages (http://www.kidzone.ws/tracers/). Custom-design your own tracer pages for students to practice specific letters or words (for example, student names, color words) or select pretyped text.

- Students will have fun practicing letter and number formation with the free version of the BT Handwriting app (http://buildandteach.com/Educational_Applications/bthandwriting.html).

- The free Hooked on Phonics Learn to Read app (http://apps.hookedonphonics.com/#) gets an update for twenty-first century learners. This interactive reading app uses phonics to teach students to read simple text.

- Inspire students to write with an abundance of child-friendly writing prompts at Kids Play and Create (http://www.kidsplayandcreate.com/50-positive-creative-writing-topics-for-kids/) and Can Teach (http://www.canteach.ca/elementary/prompts.html).

- Word walls can be an interactive way to help students identify sight words. Find word wall activities and specific ideas for special education at these sites: (http://www.teachingfirst.net/wordwallact.htm) and (http://specialed.about.com/od/wordwalls/a/morewordwalls.htm).

- The Have Fun Teaching website (https://www.havefunteaching.com/worksheets/reading-worksheets/kwl-and-kwhl-worksheets/) offers many variations on the basic K-W-L—for know, want to know, and learned—chart, including several thematic versions.

- Children can complete story maps online at ReadWriteThink (www.readwritethink.org/files/resources/interactives/storymap/).

- Student Handouts (http://www.studenthandouts.com/graphicorganizers.htm) provides a sampling of printable writing and reading graphic organizers.

- Education Place (http://www.eduplace.com/graphicorganizer/) features printable diagrams for several graphic organizers. Teachers can customize one of fourteen organizers at Worksheets Works.com (http://www.worksheetworks.com/miscellanea/graphic-organizers.html).

- Find books centered on students' interests with thematic book lists at Reading Rockets (http://www.readingrockets.org/books/booksbytheme).

- Browse student-selected children's literature at the International Literacy Association (http://www.literacyworldwide.org/get-resources/reading-lists/childrens-choices-reading-list).

Key Terms

executive functioning: How the brain sorts, categorizes, and arranges information.

goal planning: The brain's ability to follow logical steps to meet a goal.

metacognition: The ability to think about one's own thinking.

motor control: Coordination between the brain and the body to produce movement.

self-monitoring: One's ability to check for understanding and meaning while reading.

sensory processing: How an individual experiences stimulation (sight, sounds, smells, tactile input) around him.

theory of mind: The theory that suggests that students with ASD struggle to understand the feelings and perspectives of others.

thinking flexibility: The brain's ability to shift the way it approaches an activity and to adapt to changes in expectations.

working memory: Short-term memory within the brain that allows students to recall the steps within a task.

5 Turning Minds On: Actively Engaging Students

It's math time in Mrs. Jordan's preschool classroom. Today, the children are learning how to sort items. The lesson focuses on three ways to sort items: by size, by color, and by shape. The class looks on as Mrs. Jordan shows picture cards of school items. She calls on individual students to share with the class how they would sort the items, and then she repeats the process with a new set of cards. Mrs. Jordan begins the fourth card of the lesson. Although most of the students are sitting quietly, only some watch the teacher's movements. Many others appear disinterested. One student seems particularly distracted. Kimberly is watching the screen saver on the classroom computer change to random photographs of places and animals. When the screen saver image changes again, Kimberly runs to the computer. "It's a dog! It's a dog!" she yells. "My dog, Pepper, runs like this," Kimberly announces to the class. Immediately, Kimberly is on her hands and knees crawling under the classroom desks. The other students laugh as Mrs. Jordan begins to chase Kimberly around the room.

What Is Student Engagement?

Engagement is more than "hands-on"; it is also "minds-on." In other words, when students are thinking, feeling, or doing, they are engaged. Observable and unobservable behaviors are associated with student engagement, but how a student engages in learning can vary. Children can show engagement in some of the ways listed in table 5.1 that follows.

Although it can be difficult to identify every behavior of a student engaged in learning, it is fairly easy to recognize a student who is disinterested in learning. In the opening example in this chapter, Kimberly is obviously disengaged in the teacher's instruction. Instead, she is focused on the screen saver on the computer, which leads to disruptive classroom behavior. When teachers take steps to draw in students with ASD, instruction is more purposeful. This chapter will discuss specific ways to make learning more engaging for students with ASD.

Engaging Young Students with ASD

It is widely documented that students who are more engaged in school learn more. Given their learning difficulties, students with ASD, especially, benefit from instruction that is active and engaging. Students' specific strengths and weaknesses also play a huge part in designing interesting lessons for students with ASD. This is why it is so important to get to know students with ASD.

Using students' interests and learning styles helps to draw in students with ASD because it builds a natural curiosity about school. Most students want to participate more in school when activities are related to things they enjoy. Similarly, teachers who use students' interests can establish connections with students. Having a good rapport with students with ASD creates a sense of trust. This kind of trusting relationship is valuable when these students are expected to try activities that are outside of their comfort zones.

The Importance of Interests

Like many children who come to school, students with ASD want to feel valued. Building relationships with teachers and peers is a good way to help these students feel like part of the class community. Acknowledging students' interests is one way to make students feel included.

In her journal article about promoting learning through pretend play, Noriko Porter points out that it is not unusual for students with ASD to have one or two highly focused interests. In fact, it can be difficult for students

Table 5.1 Examples of Behavior Showing Student Engagement

Type of Engagement	Example Behavior
Thinking	• Asking and answering questions
	• Making connections with previous learning
	• Focusing on the speaker
Feeling	• Showing excitement or interest in a topic
	• Expressing agreement or disagreement
	• Communicating empathy for characters in a story
Doing	• Raising hand
	• Completing work
	• Reading aloud
	• Creating projects

with ASD to concentrate in school because of their intense interests. As a result, using interests to motivate students with ASD requires careful consideration. It is impossible for every task in school to be centered on students' interests. This is why teachers must work hard to find a balance between preferred interests and other school tasks.

Identifying Students' Interests

Identifying what a student with ASD likes is usually simple. They talk, draw, and write about their interests. Some interests are very unusual, such as television remotes or vacuum cleaners. Other interests are common among young children with and without ASD. For example, many preschool-age students like trains, dinosaurs, vehicles, and electronics. According to a study by Tony Attwood, the difference is that the intensity of the interest is much more pronounced for children with ASD. Although many children enjoy playing games on an adult's mobile phone, a child with ASD might spend hours memorizing the features and model numbers of dozens of mobile phones. Students with ASD who have intense interests will find ways to include their favorites in every conversation despite the questions asked or the responses given. In cases where it might be more difficult to identify students' interests, these are some suggestions to consider:

- Schedule a show-and-ask. Set up a show-and-ask afternoon. Allow students to bring in a favorite object from home. Encourage students to ask questions about their peers' possessions.

- Incorporate icebreaker games in instruction. During the first few weeks of school, consider including some simple icebreaker games in the daily schedule (see the Technology Resources section of this chapter for icebreaker game suggestions). Not only will this allow students to share

likes and dislikes, but it will also reveal common interests among students.

- Provide time for freewriting and drawing. Give students weekly opportunities to write and draw about the things that are important to them. Be a quiet observer during this time and encourage students to share their work with the class. For children who are not yet writing, offer to write a label or caption for their pictures. Encourage students to write at least the first initial of their first name and, eventually, their entire name on their drawing.

- Use interest inventories. Interest inventories allow students to write, draw, or talk in response to sentence starters or questions about their interests. Teachers can complete these inventories with students or send them home as a family project. Several interest inventories are available for free on the Internet. See the Technology Resources section of this chapter for suggested websites with early childhood interest inventory templates.

- Contact families. Parents often know their children best. Tap into this resource by making regular contact with families to discuss what best motivates their children with ASD.

- Just ask! Remember that students with ASD may learn and communicate differently, but they want to be appreciated just as much as typically developing students. Take the time to find the way that the student communicates best, and initiate a conversation about what he likes to do or enjoys most.

Weaving Interest into Daily Learning

Once the teacher has identified student-specific interests, these likes can be included in daily classroom learning in many ways. Teachers must be creative in using student favorites to build relationships and transfer interest to new things. Accomplishing these goals can ultimately lead to better student engagement. Authors Paula Kluth and Patrick Schwarz suggest four reasons to use children's interests to help students with ASD progress in the classroom:

- To connect with others
- To build student confidence
- To provide security
- To link academic goals

Finding common interests can help children with ASD connect with others. Sharing information about what they enjoy is a good way to encourage children with ASD to engage with other students. A withdrawn child with ASD who has an interest in sea animals might find common ground with a classmate who has a home aquarium. Grouping these children together could give both students an opportunity to learn from one another and build social skills. In early childhood classrooms, this type of reciprocal relationship is important because so much learning is done cooperatively. Identifying similarities among students can help them feel more comfortable learning together.

Giving children opportunities to showcase their interests can build their confidence. Too often in the classroom, students with ASD are labeled as helpless. Encouraging students with ASD to share their special talents or interests gives them opportunities to share their strengths with others—and the most receptive audience may not be their peers. Hunter, a child with Asperger syndrome, for example, became fascinated by the Civil War after his family visited several battlefields on vacation and bought him a set of plastic soldiers that represented the Union and Confederate armies. Hunter acquired an impressive body of knowledge about the topic that mystified most of his peers, but his teacher arranged for him to talk with a junior high school teacher who taught about the Civil War. The teacher's support of his interest resulted in a lifelong interest that he pursued by enrolling in Gettysburg College (near the location of one of the Civil War's most important battles). In this way, students with ASD can grow their self-esteem.

For many students with ASD, interests offer a sense of security. The typical classroom can be an overwhelming place for a child with ASD. Engaging in interests or talking about favorites can be very comforting for children with ASD. Suppose that a child with ASD has a stuffed animal collection. Allowing the child to bring a stuffed toy to be a "reading buddy" could make the student feel less anxious in stressful classroom situations. When students feel safe in the classroom, they are better able to focus on learning.

Linking interests with academic classroom goals can be a valuable strategy. Consider a three-year-old student who enjoys talking about her tricycle. Think about how this child might be more engaged in learning if the teacher selected stories that featured tricycles, used photos of tricycles to label shapes or colors, or included tricycle clip art in student worksheets. Although it can be difficult initially, incorporating interests in students' learning can have a powerful impact on building and maintaining engagement.

Dealing with Perseveration

Others sometimes see the interests of students with ASD as obsessions. Perseveration is intense focus on specific topics of interest. Often, teachers or family members may attempt to limit or even eliminate student exposure to interests to avoid perseveration. In school, interest perseveration can be both an asset and a distraction. Consider the student who likes to use computers. He can type sight words and manipulate a mouse better than any student in his kindergarten class. However, when it is time to transition to math class, it can be difficult to engage the student in a new activity.

Because a little perseveration can be beneficial, it is important to have a plan for managing it in the classroom. As with other characteristics of ASD, teachers can control perseveration by establishing structure in the classroom. It is important that students understand when and how often they can talk about or engage in preferred interests in the classroom. In addition, it is a good idea to have a designated space for these activities. These precautions help to set boundaries for perseverations, making interests less restrictive within the classroom.

Exploring Sensory Needs

For many students with ASD, sensory input has a significant influence on learning. How students with ASD process the sights, sounds, smells, and textures around them can affect their focus tremendously. If sensory experiences are under- or overstimulating, students with ASD can be easily distracted. As such, teachers must learn to read sensory needs cues from their students with ASD and offer appropriate outlets for meeting these needs.

In some cases, addressing the sensory needs of students with ASD can be effortless. If a child is fixated on the computer, for instance, preparing the child for the change and then simply turning the monitor off is one option. In other cases, it can be much more difficult to eliminate a sensory distraction. For example, the smell of lunch cooking in the school cafeteria is a much more complex distraction to address.

In addition to adjustments to the physical class environment, there are a number of sensory tools available for students with ASD. Depending on the needs of the student, these tools are designed to increase or reduce sensory input, allowing students to focus more on instruction. Table 5.2 identifies common sensory tools for young learners with ASD.

Using Movement in Class

Sensory needs can often be addressed through movement. Many young students need to move frequently to stay engaged in learning. Movement is especially important to students

Table 5.2 Common Sensory Tools for Young Learners with ASD

Sensory Tools	Tool Description	Tool Purpose
Weighted vest	Vest with light weights sewn into the vest lining	Provides constant pressure to the torso; the feeling of being swaddled can be comforting to many children with ASD
Fidget toy	Small handheld toy with interlocking parts that move or squeeze together	Allows students to keep their hands moving while listening or speaking
Foot bands	A large rubber band that fits around the front two legs of a desk or small table	Gives students a way to move their feet without leaving their seat
Sensory seating cushions	A large plastic cushion filled partially with air; seating cushions may have one side with raised bumps or bristles	Encourages frequent movement as students maintain balance while sitting on the cushion; sensory input is also provided through cushion textures
Chewy teethers	Soft plastic teethers with sensory textures (ridges, raised waves, bumps, and so on)	Offers an appropriate outlet for students who place items in their mouths
Pencil weights	Small weights that fit around a standard pencil	Encourages proper pencil grip and appropriate pressure in writing
Earmuffs	Wireless headphones	Help students block out classroom noise

with ASD because it can help them regulate their body's stimulation. When students with ASD feel stressed, movement can help them feel more safe and comfortable.

In his book about brain-focused teaching, Eric Jensen asserts that movement can benefit many students by reinforcing learning concepts, enhancing recall skills, and improving learner enthusiasm and engagement. By incorporating movement into the school day, teachers can increase the amount of oxygen in children's brains, which in turn can stimulate learning. In fact, many neurologists believe that there are similarities between how the brain processes physical activity and how the brain learns. Being aware of the connection between movement and learning can help you support student achievement. Consider the following simple ways to incorporate movement into the school day:

- Break lessons into segments and teach in various spaces in the room (such as on a carpeted area, near the desks, in the reading area, and so on). Introduce the big ideas of a math lesson in the large-group area, move students to their desks for independent practice, and organize students in partner groups for concept review.

- Provide scheduled breaks for movement throughout the school day. Take ten minutes to do exercise activities, dance routines, or active games. Danielle Wadsworth and her colleagues found that these type of movement breaks during the preschool day did not disrupt students' learning, but rather improved transitions between class activities.

- Set up movement stations around the classroom. Create math centers that allow students to practice counting to ten as they do toe touches, jumping jacks, or bunny hops.

- Incorporate activities that encourage students to coordinate movement across their bodies. Examples of this include playing patty-cake or bending at the waist and touching your toes with the opposite hand. These cross-lateral movements improve brain function and are challenging and fun for students (see *Transition Tips and Tricks for Teachers* by Jean Feldman for more examples).

- Teach students to use slow, controlled movements, such as stretching or yoga, to calm themselves when they feel frustrated or upset. Incorporate a stretch time before a daily rest period to teach students how to settle their bodies and minds prior to quiet time.

Learning Styles and ASD

All students have different learning strengths. When teachers are aware of how their students learn best, educators are able to plan lessons that engage students. In his article about learning styles and autism, Stephen Edelson suggests that students with ASD typically present with one of three learning styles: visual, auditory, or hands-on (kinesthetic). Visual learners depend on what they see to learn best, while auditory learners rely more on what they hear. Hands-on learners learn best through active participation in an activity.

Most early childhood educators use a combination of these three learning styles in daily instruction. In a single lesson, students might identify letters (visual), listen for letter sounds (auditory), and move letter tiles to build three-letter words (hands-on). Consequently, students who can gain knowledge through multiple styles will have greater opportunities to learn in school. Yet as Stephen Edelson points out, students with ASD may only have one learning style and often rely on that one style to access new information.

Visual Learning

ASD advocate Temple Grandin has described her interaction with words as a series of pictures. In her book *Thinking in Pictures,* Grandin discusses translating spoken words into pictures. Many young students with ASD also possess visual strengths. This is why so many interventions for students with ASD are based on visual cues. Schedules, reward charts, and token boards are all dependent on visual input.

To support visual learners, teachers should organize a room that is image and print rich, but not visually distracting. Whenever possible, images and text should be paired together to help students with ASD create meaningful understanding. Lessons should be infused with many opportunities to draw and write about their learning. Additionally, books and other print materials should be used to illustrate and reinforce new information. Visual learners may benefit from technology resources, such as computers or tablets, that relay information via a screen.

Auditory Learning

Communication delays are characteristic of ASD. These delays may affect verbal speech and/or language processing. Although many students with ASD can hear words that are said to them, the meaning of those words may be unclear. This language barrier influences how students process what they hear. If students struggle to make sense of what the teacher says, it will be very difficult for them to complete learning tasks.

Nonetheless, some students with ASD have minimum communication delays and learn well through auditory experiences. Students with auditory strengths thrive when teachers provide explanations and descriptions of

concepts. Furthermore, class discussions of ideas are also helpful to students who learn through hearing. These experiences allow students to hear themselves and others talk about important information.

Hands-on Learning

For many teachers, engaging learning means learning that is hands on. It is easy to assume that when students are busy doing a task that they are also busy learning something. However, not every hands-on assignment captures students' attention and promotes skill development. To be effective, hands-on learning must be meaningful to students. It has to inspire students to explore ideas and concepts more deeply.

When matched appropriately with students' learning styles, hands-on learning can be beneficial for students with ASD. However, students with ASD who are especially sensitive to sensory input may not respond as well to hands-on assignments. For example, a child who has aversions to smells or textures probably would not enjoy forming letters in shaving cream. Conversely, students with ASD who seek sensory stimulation may be more engaged with hands-on work. A student who enjoys applying and feeling pressure would most likely enjoy making shapes from clay.

Planning Engaging Lessons

Planning engaging tasks for students with ASD takes time. Teachers must get to know their students and use strengths and needs to direct class instruction. Review how this information is used to plan the following lesson example. Then, use the questions in the Student Engagement Matrix (figure 5.1) to decide how interests, sensory needs, movement, and learning styles could be used to engage a student with ASD in your classroom.

Lesson topic: Identifying /t/

Student's interests: Rocco loves animals. His mother takes him to the zoo every week, and he has many animal picture books that he carries with him to school each day.

The teacher will use this interest to help Rocco generalize the sound /t/. When introducing the sound and letter, the teacher will show picture cards with items that begin with /t/. Interspersed among these pictures will be illustrations of animals that begin with /t/ (turtle, tiger, turkey, toad, and so on). Rocco will be asked to identify some of these animals during the lesson.

Sensory needs: Rocco has difficulty sitting in the large-group area. He says that the carpet feels itchy on his hands and legs.

The teacher will offer Rocco a chair and a fidget toy during the lesson to help him remain focused and on task.

Movement: Rocco needs to move frequently (every five to seven minutes) to stay interested in class activities.

The teacher can ask students to pantomime objects that begin with /t/ (toothbrush, tongue, telephone, toe, and so on) while producing the /t/ sound. Or the teacher could list the names of several objects and have Rocco and his peers stand up when a named object begins with /t/.

Learning styles: Rocco seems more engaged in class when he can both see and hear information.

The teacher will use a fun, interactive letter T song and video during the lesson to reinforce the /t/ sound. One example is available from Have Fun Teaching (http://www.havefun teaching.com/videos/alphabet-videos/letter-t-video).

Figure 5.1 Student Engagement Matrix

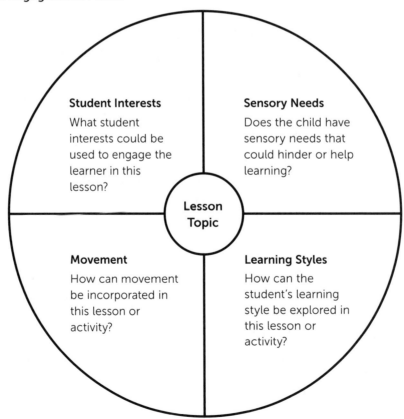

Setting Up an Engaging Environment

Students will respond differently to teaching methods, so how to best engage learners can vary from student to student. The unique characteristics of students with ASD, especially, require thoughtful planning. Although the organization of class lessons is important, teachers also must think about the type of learning environment they create for students. Because of their unique characteristics, students with ASD deserve special consideration when planning instruction.

To establish an engaging learning environment for students with ASD, librarian trainer and consultant Barbara Klipper advises taking a departure from the standard three Rs of reading, writing, and arithmetic, and instead using a different three Rs: routine, repetition, and redundancy. Students with ASD often feel more comfortable when their environment is predictable. Establishing a routine with expected activities provides this type of predictability. Repetition of task helps to create a sense of security for students and can create a level of confidence in skills as well. Further, redundancy, which many teachers may try to avoid, can actually support the learning of students with ASD. Providing multiple opportunities for students to learn and practice skills can help students with ASD better understand concepts and retain skills. The following are additional ways to offer students with ASD an engaging classroom environment.

- Adapt class assignments to meet individual students' needs. Provide multiple opportunities for students with ASD to follow their own learning process. Differentiate assignments so that students feel challenged, but not frustrated. Teaching a lesson on triangles, a preschool teacher might differentiate instruction by having some students trace a triangle outline, some draw the shape independently, and others sketch an example of a triangle shape found in the classroom. While planning differentiated assignments, be careful to match assignments to students' needs. Be mindful that some young students with ASD may need more advanced work to be engaged in learning.

- Provide choice. As often as possible, provide students with options for how they can complete assignments. Use technology, the arts, and social interaction to showcase students' learning. For example, suppose you ask students to share about their favorite foods. Students can do this through a conversation, by drawing or painting, or by making a clay model. Initiate conversations about student work and pay attention to how students learn best.

- Consider students' learning styles. Students respond differently to different instruction. Determine how each student with ASD learns best and incorporate teaching methods that focus on that style of learning. Be creative in how you address learning styles. Integrate technology, movement, and social interaction as often as possible.

- Monitor students' understanding. Younger students are not always quick to say what they do not understand. This is a skill that is even more difficult for students with ASD. If students are confused by a lesson, they will become disengaged quickly. Take frequent "temperature readings" of class understanding. Students can use a thumbs-up (I understand completely), a sideways thumb (I understand some, but not completely), or a thumbs-down (I'm confused) to indicate their level of understanding.

- Connect class learning to daily living. Students will be more engaged when learning is meaningful. Help students with

ASD see the link between what they do in class and daily tasks or preferred activities. For example, show how paying attention to and deciphering environmental print comes in handy at the grocery store when they search for favorite food items.

- Make the classroom emotionally safe. School is a place to learn, and students learn through their mistakes. Create a class environment where students can make mistakes without being teased or laughed at by teachers or classmates. Give children the option of using a signal or sign for "I don't know/understand" when a task is too difficult. Students who feel safe to make mistakes will take risks in their learning, creating ongoing engagement.

Making the classroom an engaging place for students with ASD is a challenge. However, getting to know these students' strengths, needs, and interests is the first step in making learning active.

Strategies That Engage Students with ASD in Learning

The following strategies are additional ways to build engagement in students with ASD in daily classroom activities.

Choral Response

Why Use This Strategy?

Students with ASD can be easily distracted in a busy classroom. Common objects or even peers in the learning environment can divert the attention of these learners. Once attention and interest are lost, it is almost impossible to reengage students with ASD.

Choral response encourages all students to reply to the teachers' questions. As Ann Blackwell and Tim McLaughlin point out in their journal article that explores choral response, by using this strategy, each student

has time to process and think about questions before providing a response. Students are more likely to be engaged in learning because everyone is accountable for participating in the lesson.

How Does This Strategy Work?

- Designate a hand signal or motion to determine when students will listen and think and when they will respond to your question. Possible hand signals could include a closed and open hand, touching the ear and then the mouth, or hands on shoulders and then hands on hips.

- Review these hand signals with students. Practice using the signal with basic questions. (For example: "What color is a banana?" or "How much is two plus two?") Have students practice listening and thinking first, then answering together when you give the response signal.

- Integrate the choral response strategy into instruction. First, state a question while using the listen-and-think signal. Provide appropriate wait time while holding this signal. Next, show the response signal, and have students say their answers aloud together.

- Continue the process with additional questions throughout the lesson.

Teacher Tips

- For this strategy, use questions that have short responses. Short phrases and single-word responses work best. Try this strategy in math lessons as well. Ask students to identify numerals or provide the answer to simple computation facts.

- Be sure to review the appropriate volume level for responses. Students should use a quiet, inside voice to answer questions.

- When students become proficient with this strategy, allow them to assume the teacher role and ask questions of their peers.

- Monitor student responses. If students are making many mistakes, implement reteaching strategies. Use small-group remediation for individual students who may be struggling with a lesson objective or skill.

- Remember to give students plenty of positive feedback for observing the hand signals and responding correctly.

Relevant IFSP or IEP Goals

Consider whether or not the following goals might be appropriate for children with ASD who are participating in choral response.

- Preschool—When shown zero to ten numeral flash cards, student will respond with the correct number in eight out of ten opportunities.

- Kindergarten—When shown color-word flash cards, student will respond with the correct color name in eight out of ten opportunities.

- First or second grade—When shown addition flash cards, student will respond with the correct answer in eight out of ten opportunities.

Response Cards

Materials

Index cards
Marker
Photos or images

Why Use This Strategy?

It can be difficult to encourage young students with ASD to participate in class. The fast pace of school routines along with distractions within the environment can make the classroom overwhelming.

Response cards offer a way for students with ASD to become active learners. Ann

Blackwell and Tim McLaughlin found that, when used during whole-group instruction, response cards engage the majority of the class and provide teachers with instant feedback on students' learning.

How Does This Strategy Work?

- Decide how students will respond. Response cards work best for questions with fixed answers (such as *yes/no, a/b/c/d, right/left, happy/not sure/sad,* or *true/false*).

- On index cards, use words or symbols to illustrate possible student responses. See the following photos of sample response cards.

- In a large-group setting, ask students to respond to questions by showing their response cards in front of them.

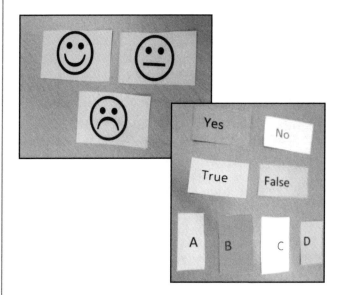

Teacher Tips

- Remember that students with ASD thrive on structure. Make sure to prepare and organize response cards prior to the lesson. Practice with the response cards before beginning the lesson.

- If the response cards are not going to be used during a period of more than five minutes, collect them or ask students to store them in a desk or cubby. The longer the response cards lay idle, the greater the potential for them to become a distraction for students.

- Use a signal or gesture so that students know when to show their response cards. This will give every student an equal chance to respond thoughtfully.

- Whenever possible, involve students in making the response cards. Allowing students to create the response cards gives them more ownership in the process of using them in class.

- Consider laminating response cards for future use.

- For responses that have just two choices, such as *yes/no*, you can make a two-sided response card attached to a paint stirrer or ruler. That way, the child can just flip it around to participate.

Relevant IFSP or IEP Goals

Consider whether or not the following goals might be appropriate for children with ASD who are using response cards.

- Preschool—Using *yes/no* response cards, student will indicate correctly whether a word begins with /b/ in four out of five opportunities.

- Kindergarten—Using yes/no response cards, student will indicate correctly whether an item is living in four out of five opportunities.

- First or second grade—Using yes/no response cards, student will indicate correctly whether a number from zero to fifty is odd in four out of five opportunities.

Priming

Why Use This Strategy?

Predictability and routine are important to students with ASD. When these learners know what to expect in the classroom, it can reduce anxiety and improve focus.

Priming exposes students to new information prior to whole-group, direct instruction. It can help children with ASD if they preview the information or activity in a low-demand environment—perhaps at home or individually in the classroom. Students get an opportunity to practice skills before they need to apply them. Such repetition of instruction can increase students' understanding and confidence. In addition, Lynn Kern Koegel and colleagues found that priming not only improved academic performance, but also decreased problem behaviors in the classroom.

How Does This Strategy Work?

- Select students who can benefit from small-group instruction.

- Focus on a new concept or skill that you will introduce to the whole class in the near future.

- Use techniques that best match students' strengths to introduce the new concept or skill. Provide opportunities for students to have guided and independent practice with the skill.

An example might be asking parents to read a book at home with the child several times, discussing the characters and story, before the whole class reads the book.

Teacher Tips

- Take into consideration the difficulty of the skill or concept when deciding how far in advance to use priming. Some skills may need more than just a few days of exposure.

- When students excel in a new topic or skill, highlight their success during the whole-group lesson. Encourage these students to participate by answering questions or illustrating the concept to peers.

- Communicate to parents when you use priming in the classroom. Provide information, homework, or practice ideas for families so that they can help reinforce the concept or skill in the home.

Relevant IFSP or IEP Goals

Consider whether or not the following goals might be appropriate for children with ASD who are exposed to priming.

- Preschool—With teacher prompting, the student will state at least one item from home that begins with the letter of the day, once per day for three consecutive days.

- Kindergarten—With teacher prompting, the student will state verbally at least one personal connection to a story read to him, once per day for three consecutive days.

- First or second grade—With teacher prompting, the student will state at least one similarity between herself and a character in a story read aloud to her, once per day for three days.

Minimodels

Materials

Varies depending on tool modeled

Why Use This Strategy?

In early childhood classrooms, routines are used to teach many functional skills. Calendar time, for instance, is a routine used in many primary classrooms. Because students with ASD often thrive on routine, minimodel lessons are a good opportunity to focus on developing skills.

Minimodels are small replicas of classroom tools. Minimodels give students with ASD an opportunity to follow the steps of the classroom routine while being wholly engaged in learning.

How Does This Strategy Work?

- Select a daily classroom routine that reviews or teaches skills (for example, calendar time, proofreading the morning letter, sight-word or math-fact review games, and so on).

- Develop a look-alike, minimodel of the classroom tool used in the routine. For example, you could make a smaller version of the classroom calendar, complete with moveable date, day, and month pieces. In this way, a student with ASD could manipulate the individual calendar as you lead morning routines with the classroom calendar.

- Have students use their models to follow routines throughout the day.

Teacher Tips

- Whenever possible, create minimodels for multiple students in the classroom. This allows students to work together throughout the routine.

- The minimodel does not need to be an exact reproduction of the actual tool. Be creative in developing the model. A handheld whiteboard with markers may provide enough support to keep students engaged during the lesson. With this type of resource, students could complete practice problems or activities along with the teacher from their desks or carpet space.

- Provide students with direct instruction on how to use the minimodel before using it in the routine. Also, encourage students to reference your use of the classroom tool as they use their minimodels.

- Collaborate with other teachers to use minimodels in other classes as well, including library, music, and physical education classes.

Relevant IFSP or IEP Goals

Consider whether or not the following goals might be appropriate for children with ASD who are using minimodels.

- Preschool—Given a minimodel manipulative, the student will correctly say the day of the week in nine out of ten opportunities over the course of two school weeks.

- Kindergarten—Given a minimodel manipulative, the student will correctly say the month of the year in nine out of ten opportunities over the course of two school weeks.

- First or second grade—Given a minimodel manipulative, the student will correctly say the date on the calendar in nine out of ten opportunities over the course of two school weeks.

Quick Draws

Materials

Paper

Pencils or crayons

Why Use This Strategy?

Students with ASD are often visual learners. When these students are able to picture in their minds words that are said or read, they can retain and process information better, and learning is more engaging. This concept of drawing a personal interpretation of information and text was first developed by Jerome Harste and his colleagues in their book *Creating Classrooms for Authors.*

Quick draws are just what their name implies—a quick drawing of the information that students have heard or read. After drawing, students should discuss their work to show understanding of ideas.

How Does This Strategy Work?

- Introduce a topic or idea. Hint: The quick draw strategy works best when paired with a lesson that presents multiple facts or ideas. Science and history lessons usually work best.

- Ask students guiding questions about what they heard. Sample guiding questions and prompts follow.

- Give students paper to draw relevant images of what comes to mind while you lead the lesson. They may also draw pictures after a lesson.

- Have students describe their picture to a teacher, a partner, or the class.

Sample Guiding Questions and Prompts

What do you remember about what you read or heard?

Show me what _____ looks like.

Where might you see _____?

What was the most important part (main idea) of the story or lesson?

What is important about _____?

Draw a picture to explain _____ to a friend.

Why do you think we are learning about _____?

Practical Strategies for Supporting Young Learners with Autism Spectrum Disorder

- Model this strategy with students before they practice independently. Show them the difference between examples and nonexamples of drawings.

- Quick draws can also be used to introduce a lesson. Give the topic of the lesson (for example, animal habitats), and ask students to use prior knowledge to sketch what they already know about it.

- You can also use this strategy in literacy activities. Ask students to draw various elements of the story structure (for example, setting, characters, or problem/solution) after they read a story or after a story is read to them.

- For younger students, an alternative to drawing is using modeling clay. Have students model shapes or images to show their understanding.

Relevant IFSP or IEP Goals

Consider whether or not the following goals might be appropriate for children with ASD who are participating in Quick Draw lessons.

- Preschool—Using the quick draw as a visual prompt, the student will describe his picture with five or more words in two out of three opportunities over three consecutive days.

- Kindergarten—Using the quick draw as a visual prompt, the student will state the main idea of a story read aloud in two out of three opportunities over three consecutive days.

- First or second grade—Using the quick draw as a visual prompt, the student will state the main idea of the science lesson correctly in two out of three opportunities over three consecutive days.

The Pop-a-Thought Strategy
Why Use This Strategy?

When students are able to explain and describe what they know, learning is more lasting. This is why classroom discussions are so valuable. However, it can be easy for young students with ASD to become disengaged if they are not encouraged to contribute to the discussion.

The Pop-a-Thought strategy allows all members of the classroom to add to the discussion in a quick and personally relevant way. This technique gives each child an opportunity to relate to the material being taught and share their understanding or interpretation of the topic.

How Does This Strategy Work?

- Select a topic of discussion.

- Allow two to three minutes wait time prior to collecting student responses. Encourage students to think of two or three responses just in case others share the same idea first.

- Ask each student to contribute a short sentence or phrase to the discussion. Have students add to the discussion in a round-robin fashion.

- After all students offer a response, provide feedback on a sample of student responses.

Teacher Tips

- Consider using a procedure that allows students to participate randomly (for example, by selecting craft sticks with student names). This way, students will have to stay engaged for longer periods of time.

- Use the Pop-a-Thought strategy to build focus prior to beginning a lesson. For example, start a math lesson by asking each student to name one way to make ten, or begin a health lesson by asking each student to name a way to exercise.

- Use the Pop-a-Thought strategy to help students work on distinguishing among *wh-* questions (who, what, where, when, and why). When asking *wh-* questions, remind students of the type of response that is required (for example, who—a person, what—a thing, where—a place, and so on).

- Create a safe environment for sharing. Assist students in offering relevant ideas and encourage further thinking when the response is not on target.

Relevant IFSP or IEP Goals

Consider whether or not the following goals might be appropriate for children with ASD who are using the Pop-a-Thought strategy.

- Preschool—Given a topic, the student will add one relevant comment to a group discussion on four out of five consecutive school days.

- Kindergarten—Given a topic, the student will add at least one relevant comment to a group discussion on four out of five consecutive school days.

- First or second grade—Given a topic, the student will add at least two relevant comments to a group discussion on four out of five consecutive school days.

The Classroom Detective Strategy
Why Use This Strategy?

Movement makes learning more active. Students with ASD, especially, may need regular physical activity to regulate themselves and manage sensory input. These learners can also benefit from learning that is self-paced.

Being a classroom detective is a fun, interactive way for students to demonstrate understanding. This activity encourages students to move around the room as they look for examples of specific classroom topics or ideas.

Sample Detective Searches

What do you remember about what you read or heard? Please look for items that . . .

begin/end with the letter _____.

are shaped like a _____ (square, rectangle, and so on).

are living things.

have four sides.

have a _____ (hard, soft, smooth) texture.

are about 1 inch long/longer than 1 inch.

rhyme with _____.

have a _____ (letter/number) on them.

are made from _____ (plastic, wood, paper).

are people/place/thing nouns.

How Does This Strategy Work?

- Select a topic or subject area around which to design a classroom detective search. See the sample detective searches that follow.

- Review the focus of the search, and show both examples and nonexamples of evidence.

- Encourage students to move around the room to search for examples or "clues."

- Monitor student progress and provide feedback or assistance as needed.

- After several minutes of searching, have students gather together to talk about their findings.

Teacher Tips

- Remind students to behave like detectives. Encourage them to work quietly and carefully.

- Ask older students to record examples or clues from their search.

- For some searches, it may be necessary to place specific examples in the classroom environment in advance.

- When appropriate, consider moving the classroom detective search outside.

- Provide students with a warning before closing the search. Students with ASD, in particular, will need notice before ending the task.

- As a closing activity, use the Pop-a-Thought strategy (see page 91) to allow students to share one example they found in their searches.

Relevant IFSP or IEP Goals

Consider whether or not the following goals might be appropriate for children with ASD who are using the Classroom Detective strategy.

- Preschool—Student will name correctly three blue items found in the classroom environment over three consecutive days.

- Kindergarten—Student will name correctly three items that begin with /s/ in the classroom environment over three consecutive days.

- First or second grade—Student will name correctly three noun items found in the classroom environment over five consecutive days.

Technology Resources for Engaging Learners with ASD

- View samples of student interest inventories on Pinterest (https://www.pinterest.com/explore/student-interest-survey/).

- Teachers Pay Teachers (https://www.teacherspayteachers.com/Browse/Grade-Level/PreK-K/Search:interest+surveys) also has several free or inexpensive picture-based interest and reading surveys.

- Icebreaker games can be a fun way to help students share interests. Great Group Games (http://www.greatgroupgames.com/icebreaker-games-for-kids.htm) and Ultimate Camp Resource (http://www.ultimatecampresource.com/site/camp-activities/camp-games.html) have several game ideas for young students.

- Fun and Function (https://funandfunction.com/) is an online catalog of sensory needs products for students.

- Explore Dr. Jean.org (http://drjean.org/) for several ideas to engage young learners. Videos, song lyrics, and cross-lateral activities are available for immediate classroom use.

- Education.com (http://www.education.com/magazine/article/10-activities-children-autism/) has suggestions for games and activities to engage students with ASD in classroom activities.

- JumpStart (http://www.jumpstart.com /parents/activities/classroom-activities) has task cards for fun learning games to reinforce general classroom skills.

- Do2Learn (http://www.do2learn.com/games /learninggames.htm) provides several online games that can be incorporated with early childhood lessons.

- At The Teacher Toolkit (www .theteachertoolkit.com/index.php/tool /student-response-cards), get tips for using response cards and watch a video of an elementary classroom using response cards.

- See examples of response cards at Autism Classroom News (http://www .autismclassroomresources.com /?s=response+cards). A Google image search (https://images.google.com) will also provide several additional models. Simply type "student response cards" in the toolbar.

- Engage students by pairing movement with choral response techniques. This SchoolTube video (http://www.schooltube .com/video/10d69f44e7694a359c49 /choral%20response%20examples) shows several examples of ways to incorporate this strategy.

Key Terms

choral response: A student engagement technique that encourages students to respond to teacher questions together in chorus.

cross-lateral movements: Large movements that cross to the opposite side of the body.

engagement: The thinking, feeling, and doing that inspires focus and learning.

perseveration: Intense focus on a single item or group of items, often to the point of obsession.

priming: Pre-teaching of the skills or concepts of a lesson individually or in a small group prior to introduction to the whole class.

response cards: A set of cards with fixed responses for students to use to answer the teacher's or a peer's questions.

sensory needs: Refers to the amount of sensory (sight, sound, smell, touch) input a student needs to feel comfortable in a setting.

6 Addressing Behavioral Concerns

In art class, students in Mr. Green's class will be painting portraits. While Mr. Green leads a short lesson on how to use the supplies appropriately, Ben sings loudly and claps his hands. Mr. Green asks Ben several times to stop interrupting the class. After Mr. Green completes his minilesson, he begins to give each student paint sets to use for the project. Several students begin to paint happily. When Mr. Green gets to Ben's table, he realizes that he does not have enough paint sets to give each student his own. Four students at the last table must share two sets. Mr. Green places the first paint set down in front of Kevin, and places the second one in front of Maria, Ben's art partner for the day. Watching this, Ben becomes very angry. First, he begins to cry. Then, he stands up and walks around the room, opening cabinets and drawers in the art room. He throws paper and glue bottles onto the floor. Mr. Green asks Ben several times to return to his seat, but he refuses. Grabbing Ben's hand, Mr. Green takes Ben back to his table and directs him to sit, but Ben pulls away and grabs Maria's painting and throws it on the floor. When the principal comes into the classroom to intervene, Mr. Green explains, "Ben has been disruptive all morning, and then he started misbehaving for no reason."

Behavior as Communication

Language delays make it difficult for some students with ASD to express their wants, needs, feelings, and frustrations in words. As a result, many young students with ASD use behavior as a way to communicate. Tearing up a paper might mean "I am confused." Throwing an object could mean "I want to be first." When teachers interpret behaviors such as these appropriately, they can help students manage stressful situations. This does not mean that teachers should give students with ASD everything they want or eliminate classroom demands completely. Instead, teachers must learn to anticipate how their students with ASD will respond in situations, and use this information to shape more positive behaviors.

Types of Behavior

Before teachers can address challenging behaviors, it is helpful to identify the behavior type. The behavior type along with personal information about students can assist teachers in detecting patterns in students' actions and providing appropriate interventions. For instance, the teacher knows that Cathy flaps her hands when she feels anxious or nervous. The teacher notices that Cathy flaps her hands every time a visitor enters the classroom. During the next three weeks, the teacher prepares Cathy for classroom visitors by placing an icon on the classroom visual schedule. Doing so makes Cathy less anxious, and she begins to flap her hands less often. See table 6.1, which shows the most common behavior types and examples of each category.

Behavior Functions

Recognizing the function of a behavior is just as important as identifying the behavior type. Considering the behavior function answers the question why a student engages in a particular behavior. Consider a child with ASD who cries when told to leave the computer center. Not wanting to see the student upset, the teacher allows the child to continue to use the computer. In this instance, the behavior (crying) allows the child to get what she wants (more computer time).

Studying behavior function can help teachers improve students' behavior. Think about the example at the opening of this chapter. By engaging in challenging behavior, Ben hopes to get his own paint set. When the teacher places the paint set in front of his partner instead of in front of him, his challenging behaviors quickly escalate. There are a couple of reasons why Ben might respond in this way. Maybe he has difficulty controlling his impulses. Perhaps in some previous setting Ben has been taught that challenging behaviors result in him getting his own way. In either case, of course, this behavior is not acceptable for school. Now that the function of the behavior has been identified, Ben's teachers can begin to organize a plan to address the behavior. See figure 6.1, which describes the three most common behavior functions for students with ASD.

Table 6.1 Common Behavior Types and Examples

Challenging Behaviors	Self-Stimulating Behaviors	Self-Injurious Behaviors	Withdrawal
• Hitting others	• Flapping hands	• Hair pulling	• Crying
• Kicking others	• Mouthing objects	• Scratching self	• Playing alone
• Biting others	• Lining objects up	• Picking at scabs	• Ignoring others
• Destroying property	• Rocking back and forth	• Hitting self	• Scripting

Practical Strategies for Supporting Young Learners with Autism Spectrum Disorder

Figure 6.1 Common Functions of Behaviors

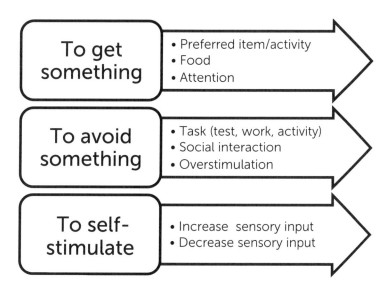

Applied behavioral analysis (ABA) uses well-established techniques to target the specific behavioral needs of students with ASD. Central to ABA therapy is the common principle that rewarding behavior will increase the likelihood that a person will repeat it. ABA uses a systematic process to shape behavior through positive reinforcement. Based on individual student needs, the teacher organizes skills in small, attainable steps reinforced with preferred activities or objects. As students master skill sets, the teacher introduces more complex goals.

ABA theory views behavior as having three parts: an antecedent, a behavior, and a consequence. Recognizing these elements can help the teacher identify the type and function of a behavior. This is why it is important that teachers learn to be observant of the events before and after the behavior. One way to do this is to use an antecedent-behavior-consequence (ABC) chart. An ABC chart gives teachers a way to record the antecedent (what happened before the behavior), the actual behavior, and the consequence (what happened in response to the behavior). Using this type of resource can help teachers study patterns in behaviors and make choices to prevent student meltdowns. Table 6.2 shows an example of an ABC chart. Review the sample entries in the table, and then use the guiding questions that follow to interpret the student's and teacher's behaviors.

Table 6.2 An Example Antecedent-Behavior-Consequence (ABC) Chart

Antecedent	Behavior	Consequence
Teacher asks the student to trace his name on the paper.	Student begins to hit children at his table.	Student goes to the time-out corner.
Music teacher asks students to sing the song they learned in class.	Student crawls under her chair.	Student must return to her classroom.
Teacher distributes paper for a drawing activity.	Student tears the paper into pieces.	Student sent to the reading center to look at books.

Each time the student is given a work demand, he engages in negative behavior. It would be a fair assumption that these activities are not preferred choices for the student. By hitting, hiding under his desk, and destroying his work, the child is communicating that he does not want to participate in these tasks. The teacher is reinforcing undesirable behavior by assigning consequences that allow the student to avoid the assigned task.

Studying students' behavior through an ABC chart can help teachers see patterns in how children respond to stressful situations. With this knowledge, teachers can predict students' behaviors more accurately and implement positive behavior strategies. Create your own ABC chart to collect data on students' behaviors in your classroom.

Teacher Responses to Behavior

How teachers respond is critical to managing behaviors. It is important to consider the child's needs and to respond in a way that builds resilience when the child is engaged in nonpreferred items and activities. However, many of the practices that can be effective with typically developing students are not always effective with students with ASD. A raised voice or simple redirection may do more to frustrate the student than shape behaviors.

Teachers, therefore, can look for alternative approaches for students with ASD.

Before developing a plan for treating students' behaviors, teachers can help by educating themselves about the challenges of the disability and how they affect young children. Being mindful of differences among students with ASD can help when crafting strategies for dealing with classroom behaviors. Behavior support plans should be tailored specifically to the needs of individual students. Having insight about individual students allows teachers to set realistic behavior expectations for students with ASD.

In his book *No More Meltdowns,* behavior consultant Jed Baker describes this process as accepting and appreciating the child. Baker suggests that this attitude is critical in addressing challenging behaviors because it helps teachers control their own frustrations and build a sense of competency in the student. Consider again the story of Ben from the opening of this chapter. Mr. Green believes that Ben has tried to disrupt the class purposely. He has not reflected on the idea that Ben's ASD might make it difficult for him to understand that he was supposed to share the paint set with Maria. Further, Mr. Green expects Ben to make this assumption on his own, despite the fact that ASD makes reading social cues difficult.

Imagine how this scene might have unfolded differently if Mr. Green had explained to the class that some students would need to share paints. Think about how Ben might have responded if Mr. Green had modeled for Ben how he could share the paint set with Maria. In this alternative scenario, both Ben and Mr. Green would most likely avoid emotional overload, and Ben would have an opportunity to rehearse a valuable social skill (sharing) with his peers.

Preventing Problem Behaviors

Teacher attitude alone, however, will not change students' behaviors. Careful planning is necessary to promote changes in the behaviors of students with ASD. As Chantal Sicile-Kira explains in her autism guide, teachers must implement strategies that substitute negative behaviors with prosocial choices called replacement behaviors. Replacement behaviors must serve the same function as the initial behavior. For example, if a student hits his classmates because he is tired of coloring, an effective replacement behavior might be to have the student ask for a break. When the student asks for a break, the teacher should praise him for his positive choice. In this way, the function of the behavior—getting a break—remains the same.

Once behaviors are identified along with the functions they serve, the student support team can develop a behavior intervention plan. The behavior intervention plan outlines specific strategies that the team will used to decrease problem behaviors and increase prosocial choices. Although the special education teacher typically writes the behavior intervention plan, the general education teacher should be able to offer input. Behavior intervention plans are written specifically for individual students, but each behavior intervention plan should have some common elements. The Individuals with Disabilities Education Act (IDEA) requires the following in a behavior intervention plan:

- Description of the targeted behavior
- Review of failed strategies to address the behavior
- List of the members of the student support team who will implement the plan
- Description of observable behavior changes and how these data will be measured
- Plan for addressing extreme problem behaviors (crisis plan)
- Strategies to share information about the behavior intervention plan between home and school
- Time line for reviewing the effectiveness of the behavior intervention plan

As the support team develops behavior interventions, it is critical to remember to keep the plan positive. Include strategies that use the student's interests and strengths to address behaviors. Make families an integral part of creating and implementing the plan. Most important, be mindful that students with ASD do not engage in challenging behaviors to hurt and frustrate others purposefully. Learn to see behavior as a language and be committed to helping students with ASD express their needs and wants appropriately. The following are other ways teachers can help students with ASD work through problem behaviors:

- **Reward positive choices.** When students make good behavior choices, the teacher should offer positive reinforcement. Students can work for a tangible prize (stickers, treats, small toys, and so on) or teacher recognition. Many students with ASD are highly motivated by a hug or high five from a respected teacher.

- **Practice, practice, practice.** Keep in mind that many students with ASD must be taught social and behavioral skills directly. Create opportunities in the classroom for students to practice these skills. Use peer models to demonstrate appropriate behaviors.

- **Share simple scenarios.** Use brief descriptions of a behavior and its consequences to coach children with ASD in appropriate responses to common situations. You can create these behavior descriptions in response to a classroom incident and accompany them with photographs, drawings, or a role play. (A sample scenario for role playing: The preschool class got a new wagon. Tanya is pulling a doll in the wagon. Gloria wants a turn to pull the new wagon. Tanya says no. Now Gloria is angry. Why is she angry?)

- **Give advance notice.** Whenever possible, let students know when there will be a change in the normal routine. Talk through these situations with students *before* they have to confront them.

- **Teach the child to share his feelings.** Encourage students with ASD to express how they are feeling. Help them to recognize when they feel stressed or need a break from a situation. Teach them ways to cope in stressful situations.

- **Be proactive.** Be aware of environmental triggers that can upset or frustrate the student. Use additional supports to help students navigate these experiences.

- **Teach routines and expectations.** Before students can engage in appropriate behaviors, they must be aware of what is expected from them. Use child-friendly resources to teach these concepts to students. Many students with ASD respond well to personalized stories about how to behave appropriately. Social Stories, a concept developed by Carol Gray, tell a narrative of how a child should respond in a social situation. Social Stories can be written on a number of topics, such as how to share toys or how to ride the school bus. Similarly, Gray's strategy of comic strip conversations uses comic-strip style illustrations and thought bubbles to help students understand what others are thinking. Understanding perspectives different from their own can help students make behavioral choices that are pleasing to others, not just themselves.

- **Make prompts concrete.** Help students with ASD start and stop tasks by giving them concrete images to visualize or act out. For example, for the child who is being too silly in class, the teacher might tell him to "throw his giggles away." Next, the child can pantomime throwing his giggles in a garbage can. Although this strategy may sound silly, many students with ASD think literally and can benefit from these very real prompts.

- **Hit the restart button.** Do not let one negative behavior destroy an entire day. Address challenging behaviors as they occur, then allow students to transition back to learning. Help students learn from mistakes without dwelling on them.

Managing Meltdowns

It has been a difficult morning drop-off at the preschool center. Byron, a four-year-old, has had a major tantrum that involved crawling under the climbing equipment and pitching blocks and toys at anyone who came nearby. Several parents observed this incident and contacted the school later that day to complain about Byron's behavior. The families demanded to know how their children would be kept safe at school. The administrator is scheduled to observe this class next week and Byron's teacher's worst fear is that he will have a meltdown while she is being evaluated.

Preventing meltdowns for children like Byron is ideal; no one wants to see any child in a frustrating situation. Certainly, teachers can put some procedures in place to decrease student stress. However, autism consultant and author Jed Baker points out in his book that even the most highly skilled teacher cannot control how her students respond and react to the world around them, and problem behaviors will occur. In these instances, it is important for teachers to be aware of ways that they can help students with ASD manage their feelings and control their behaviors. The following are some ways classroom teachers can respond to problem behaviors:

- **Avoid panic.** It can be upsetting when a child with ASD engages in disruptive or aggressive behavior. Yet if a teacher shows frustration or anger, it can intensify these challenging student behaviors. Instead, maintain a calm voice and stay in control of your emotions. When students with ASD feel out of sync, they depend on the people around them to maintain stability.

- **Use simple, clear directions.** Once a student starts to have a tantrum, the opportunity for discussion and negotiation has passed. Provide the student with simple, clear directions which express your expectations for the given time (for example, "stand up," "stop," "sit down," and so on).

- **Remove the student from the situation.** Whenever possible, try to change the environment. Often, stimuli from within the classroom can increase problem behaviors. Removing a student during times of stress can decrease sensory overload and improve focus and attention.

- **Limit outside stimulation.** If it is not possible to remove the student from the classroom, try limiting sensory input. Reduce unnecessary noise, dim the lighting, and locate comfortable seating.

- **Redirect attention.** Try to get the student to focus on something else. Use the student's interests to calm his outburst.

- **Show, don't tell.** Being in a state of anxiety and stress compromises language processing and understanding for some students with ASD. Pair visual prompts with verbal cues to help students understand expectations for behavior.

- **Reassure the child that she is safe.** Remind the child that she is safe at school. Keep a comfort toy—an item that the child can hold or hug—at school to help the student relax.

- **Ask for help.** Seek assistance from school personnel who have a rapport with the child. The student may find it easier to talk with these individuals.

From time to time, problem behaviors will happen at school. It is important that teachers address the behaviors, help students work through their frustration, and transition students directly back to their classroom activities. Remember, for many students with ASD, challenging behavior is a form of communication. When teachers are able to interpret what students with ASD are trying to say, challenging behaviors will decrease significantly. The following strategies can help students with ASD manage their behaviors in the classroom.

Strategies to Address Challenging Behaviors

First, Then Boards

Materials

Card stock

Pictures or symbols of various class activities or tasks (for example, a computer, a pencil, a paintbrush, and so on) cut from old magazines, books, or printed computer images

Hook and loop sticky-backed tape

Why Use This Strategy?

It can be difficult for a student with ASD to understand what others expect from him. Even in a structured classroom, many students with ASD struggle to internalize their daily routines. Further, changes to established schedules can create stress and anxiety for young children with ASD.

First, Then boards highlight a very small portion of a student's daily schedule. In this way, the student can see what task, activity, or work he must complete before engaging in a preferred activity. *First, Then* boards help students with ASD visualize expectations and goals.

How Does This Strategy Work?

- Select a small portion of the child's school day. If possible, choose a section of the school day that is particularly challenging for the student and that is followed by a more preferred activity.

- Use a piece of card stock as the board. Turn the paper in the landscape position. Draw a vertical line on the paper to create two equal columns. Label the left side *First* and the right side *Then*.

- Pick two pictures from the ones you have collected, to show a sequence of activities. You can use hook and loop tape to fasten the pictures to the board if you like. That way you can easily substitute different images for new tasks. On the *First* side of the board, place a picture of the task that should be completed first. On the *Then* side, place a picture of the task that should be completed next.

- Show the student with ASD the order of the tasks. Say, "First _____, then _____," so the student will be aware of task expectations. Use a nonverbal prompt (finger point) to reference the picture of the current task.

- When the *First* task is complete, assist the student in transitioning to the *Then* task.

Teacher Tips

- Consider laminating the *First, Then* board to make it more durable for daily use.

- After you state the task order, encourage the student to repeat it (for example, "First writing, then computer time"). This will help students remain aware of expectations.

- If possible, use actual photographs of the student with ASD engaged in the tasks for the *First, Then* board. Adding this personal connection will help create interest and ownership for the student.

- Demonstrate to other teachers and staff, such as special teachers and cafeteria workers, how to use the *First, Then* board with the student. This support can be helpful to a student with ASD across multiple settings.

Relevant IFSP or IEP Goals

Consider whether or not the following goals might be appropriate for children with ASD who are using the *First, Then* Boards strategy.

- Preschool—Presented with a teacher request, student will use a *First, Then* board to complete a five-minute nonpreferred activity before a preferred activity in four out of five opportunities over five consecutive days.

- Kindergarten—Presented with a teacher request, student will use a *First, Then* board to complete a ten-minute nonpreferred activity before a preferred activity in four out of five opportunities over five consecutive days.

- First or second grade—Presented with a teacher request, student will use a *First, Then* Board to complete a fifteen-minute nonpreferred activity before a preferred activity in four out of five opportunities over five consecutive days.

Visual Bracelets
Materials
Several picture representations of class expectations
Key rings
Hole punch
Laminating materials
Bracelet

Why Use This Strategy?

Verbal redirection is not always effective for students with ASD. Intense focus on other interests can cause these children to tune out teacher directions. In addition, constant repetition of class expectations can interrupt the flow of learning for the classroom.

A visual bracelet allows the student with ASD to see a pictorial reminder of teacher directions and class expectations. When students see the visual prompt, they know what they need to do to participate in the lesson and how to correct their behavior.

How Does This Strategy Work?

- Select several picture representations of class expectations. A list of suggestions for activities to illustrate follows. Pictures can be small drawings, photos, or small clip-art images.

- Selected pictures should be small, approximately one-inch by one-inch square. Laminate pictures and punch a hole in each picture.

- String together pictures on a key ring. The key ring should be attached to a form-fitting bracelet that fits comfortably around a teacher's or paraprofessional's wrist.

- During a lesson, show the student a picture card to prompt appropriate behavior. For example, if the student is lying on the carpet during story time, you would show the student the sit picture.

Teacher Tips

- Whenever possible, simply show the student the picture card without a verbal prompt. This will help students learn to correct their behavior more independently.

- Part of the appeal of visual bracelets is their versatility. Wear the bracelet throughout the day to help students with ASD comply with requests during transition and unscheduled times (for example, in hallways, in the lunchroom, and so on). Encourage staff in various settings to wear and use a visual bracelet in their classrooms.

Suggested Activities to Illustrate on the Visual Bracelet

- *Sit—child sitting in chair*
- *Listen—hand to ear*
- *Look—eyes*
- *Work—hand drawing on paper*
- *Read—book*
- *Raise hand—child with hand raised*
- *Walk—child taking steps*
- *Quiet—child with head lowered and hands folded*

Relevant IFSP or IEP Goals

Consider whether or not the following goals might be appropriate for children with ASD who are using the Visual Bracelets strategy.

- Preschool—With no more than two teacher prompts, student will attend to (eyes on speaker, body still, silent voice, hands to self) whole-group instruction for a seven-minute period in four out of five opportunities over five consecutive days.

- Kindergarten—With no more than two teacher prompts, student will attend to (eyes on speaker, body still, silent voice, hands to self) whole-group instruction for a seven-minute period in four out of five opportunities over five consecutive days.

- First or second grade—With no more than two teacher prompts, student will attend to (eyes on speaker, body still, silent voice, hands to self) whole-group instruction for a ten-minute period in four out of five opportunities over five consecutive days.

The Build a Picture Strategy
Materials
Several picture representations to represent each step of multistep school activities
Scissors

Why Use This Strategy?
Many school activities are made up of multiple steps. When students with ASD are familiar with these procedures, they are less anxious and frustrated in school. Lessening these stressful emotions can decrease problem behaviors.

The Build a Picture strategy uses puzzle pieces to represent the different steps of classroom activities. As the puzzle gets completed, so does the learning task. In this way, students with ASD can better understand expectations for specific class activities.

How Does This Strategy Work?
- Select a task that has multiple steps.

- Select a corresponding picture for the selected task. Cut the picture into pieces; there should be one piece for each step in the class activity. For example, if the class is working on a literacy activity that has writing, drawing, cutting, and pasting parts, the picture would be divided into four parts.

- Help the student associate each step with a piece of the picture puzzle. Describe each step of the task while assigning its picture piece.

- As the student completes each step, have him put the picture puzzle piece in place.

- Make sure the student continues this process until all steps in the task are done and the picture is complete.

Teacher Tips
- Use a picture of something students like to motivate them. Consider students' interests when planning for this strategy.

- Begin with activities with fewer steps. When students become comfortable with this activity, increase the number of steps.

- Prepare multiple (three-piece, four-piece, and five-piece) picture sets and have them ready for various activities throughout the day.

- Vary the size of picture pieces. Assign larger pieces to more difficult or complex assignment parts.

Relevant IFSP or IEP Goals
Consider whether or not the following goals might be appropriate for children with ASD who are using the Build a Picture strategy.

- Preschool—Student will complete two-step assignment with two or fewer teacher prompts on four out of five consecutive days.

- Kindergarten—Student will complete three-step assignment with two or fewer teacher prompts on four out of five consecutive days.

- First or second grade—Student will complete four-step assignment with two or fewer teacher prompts on four out of five consecutive days.

The On Your Spot Strategy
Why Use This Strategy?
Having a sense of boundaries can be comforting to some students with ASD. Less-structured environments can be confusing for many students with ASD, creating anxiety and frustration. These emotions commonly inspire problem behaviors for student with ASD.

The On Your Spot strategy creates a home base for students with ASD. Students can retreat to this area to regulate feelings and sensory input. In addition, this special space can remind students with ASD of behavior expectations for particular class activities.

How Does This Strategy Work?

- Assign the student with ASD a personal area in the classroom. Be sure that the area is free of as many distracting items as possible.

- When the student with ASD engages in problem behaviors or needs a few minutes to regulate his energy, use the phrase *on your spot* with the student's name in front: "Rasheed—on your spot." This should be a signal for the student to return to his personal area.

- Once the student goes to his personal area, help him complete some calming activities. For example, you might take a series of deep breaths with the student or sing or hum quietly to the child.

- As soon as the child discontinues the problem behavior, help him transition back to the activity from which he was removed.

Teacher Tips

- Use a physical object to designate the child's personal area. A carpet square, pillow, or floor mat will work well. This also makes the spot portable so that the strategy can be used in other classroom settings.

- Consider adding one or two comforting items in the student's spot. For example, a fidget toy or a soft stuffed animal can help a student with ASD calm down when under stress.

- Try using the On Your Spot strategy for students who have difficulty staying in a designated space during less structured class times (for example, carpet reading, learning centers, partner group work, and so on).

- Once problem behaviors stop, make transitioning the student back to the learning activity the first priority. Later, discuss more appropriate behavior choices with the child.

Relevant IFSP or IEP Goals

Consider whether or not the following goals might be appropriate for children with ASD who are using the On Your Spot strategy.

- Preschool—Student will sit appropriately (for example, with hands in lap, legs crossed, and facing forward) in her assigned space without visual or verbal prompting for five minutes in four out of five opportunities.

- Kindergarten—Student will sit appropriately (for example, with hands in lap, legs crossed, and facing forward) in his assigned space without visual or verbal prompting for seven minutes in four out of five opportunities.

- First or second grade—Student will sit appropriately (for example, with hands in lap, legs crossed, and facing forward) in her assigned space without visual or verbal prompting for ten minutes in four out of five opportunities.

Interruption Cards

Materials
Index cards
Marker
Box or bag for cards

Why Use This Strategy?

Students with ASD thrive on structure and routine. However, disruptions to the classroom schedule are common in early childhood classrooms. Teaching students with ASD to respond appropriately to changes in their daily routine can help them feel more comfortable in the school environment.

Like many other social and behavioral skills, students with ASD need practice managing changes to routine effectively. Interruption cards allow teachers to plan for disruptions to school routines and to provide structure and support for students with ASD as they adjust to change.

How Does This Strategy Work?

- Create a list of five to seven interruption activities. These activities should be both preferred and nonpreferred activities (for example, ten minutes of free play, five minutes of computer time, five minutes of math fact practice, ten minutes of handwriting, and so on).

- Write interruption activities on small cards and place each card in a bag or box.

- At random times throughout the school day, announce an interruption activity and select an interruption card.

- Read the interruption card to the class and adjust the class or individual visual schedule to reflect the interruption activity change. Next, lead students in beginning the interruption activity.

- Work directly with the student with ASD and explain that there has been a change to the schedule. Support the student's participation in the interruption activity as needed.

Teacher Tips

- Collaborate with the student's family to determine preferred activities for the interruption cards.

- Initially, use more preferred activity interruption cards than nonpreferred activities. This allows the student to build some coping skills before they must adjust to more unfavorable changes to routine.

- You might want to add pictures or symbols to illustrate the activity to support students with ASD.

- You may need to use direct instruction to teach students with ASD ways to cope with change appropriately. Model these strategies with all students frequently. Students with ASD may need visual and spoken prompts to manage schedule changes.

- Praise students with ASD when they respond to changes in the routine without incident.

Relevant IFSP or IEP Goals

Consider whether or not the following goals might be appropriate for children with ASD who are using the Interruption Cards strategy.

- Preschool—With visual and verbal prompts, the student will accept changes in daily school routines without engaging in problem behaviors on four out of five consecutive days.

- Kindergarten—With visual prompts, the student will accept changes in daily school routines without engaging in problem behaviors on four out of five consecutive days.

- First or second grade—Without prompting, the student will accept changes in daily school routines without engaging in problem behaviors for four out of five consecutive days.

Touch Schedules
Materials
Small items as visual cues

Why Use This Strategy?
Transitions are an important part of daily routines. Knowing when to start and stop a task builds independence and allows students to participate in many school, home, and community activities. However, transitioning can be particularly difficult for some students with ASD because of rigidity in their thinking and planning.

As researchers Janet Schmit and her colleagues explained in their journal article, using visual cues can help students with disabilities transition from activities with limited problem behaviors. A touch schedule allows students with ASD to both see and feel an object that prompts him to transition to a new activity.

How Does This Strategy Work?

- Select a small portion of the student's daily schedule.

- Select an object to represent each activity in the schedule. See the sample object cue ideas that follow.

- Five minutes before transition time, set the visual cue near the student within his line of vision. Give the verbal prompt that the student has five minutes before it is time to change activities.

- Two minutes before transition time, bring the visual cue closer to the student. Give a second verbal prompt telling students that they have two minutes before it is time to change activities.

- At transition time, give the visual object cue to the student to hold. Next, tell the student that it is time to stop and remind the student what activity comes next.

Teacher Tips

- Adjust the number of verbal prompts to match students' needs. Try to use the fewest number of verbal prompts that allow the student to transition successfully.

- Encourage the student with ASD to watch the behaviors of his peers to know how and when to transition to new tasks.

- Praise students for transitioning appropriately.

Relevant IFSP or IEP Goals

Consider whether or not the following goals might be appropriate for children with ASD who are using Touch Schedules.

- Preschool—Given verbal and visual prompts, the student will transition from school tasks and activities without problem behaviors (crying, aggression, or yelling) four out of five times over five consecutive days.

Sample Transition Object Cues

- *Writing—pencil or pen*
- *Drawing—marker or crayon*
- *Math—magnetic numbers*
- *Art—paintbrush*
- *Reading—book*
- *Physical education—ball*
- *Music—tambourine*
- *Lunch—lunch bag*
- *Dismissal—backpack*

- Kindergarten—Given visual prompts, the student will transition from school tasks and activities without problem behaviors (crying, aggression, or yelling) four out of five times over five consecutive days.

- First or second grade—Without prompting, the student will transition from school tasks and activities without problem behaviors (crying, aggression, or yelling) four out of five times over five consecutive days.

Walk and Talk Breaks

Why Use This Strategy?

The wide spectrum of sensory input combined with task demands from teachers and peers can quickly overwhelm a student with ASD. When teachers recognize signals that indicate stress overload, they can prevent many of the behaviors that accompany an emotional breakdown in students with ASD. This is why a predictable break schedule is so important to students with ASD.

Walk and Talks combine a movement break with academically focused social interaction. This strategy allows students to have a sensory break while staying engaged in learning. In addition, Walk and Talks briefly reinforce an appropriate way for students with ASD to respond to high-stress situations.

How Does This Strategy Work?

- During the Walk and Talk Break activities, adult or peer partners work with students with ASD to engage them in fast paced review activities.

- Work with the student support team to determine an appropriate amount of breaks for the student with ASD. The breaks should be spread throughout the school day.

- During one of the predetermined breaks, assign an activity for the student with ASD to complete as he walks about a designated space.

- At the end of the break, help the student return to the class activity. Assign a different activity for the next Walk and Talk Break.

The following suggestions provide an idea of activities that work well with the Walk and Talk strategy:

- Math fact review—Ask the student to answer simple addition or subtraction questions.

- Letter, number, or color recognition— Have the student identify a specified letter, number, or color within the school environment.

- Spelling word practice—Ask the student to spell common sight words.

- Flash card activities—Give the student practice with flash card tasks.

- Rhyming pairs—Challenge the student to provide a rhyming word when given a familiar word.

- Vocabulary definitions—Ask the student to define key content terms or provide the term for a common definition.

- Getting to know you questions—Give the student practice asking and answering questions about himself and others.

Teacher Tips

- The entire class can benefit from a Walk and Talk Break. Pose higher-order thinking questions to all students and give them an opportunity to discuss them as they move around the classroom or another space.

- Keep in mind that Walk and Talks do not have to include actual walking. Students can be engaged in other movement activities, including bouncing on a trampoline, running in place, dancing, or stretching movements.

- Use a timer or other signal to monitor the length of the Walk and Talk Break. Make sure that the students with ASD know how long the break will be and how they will transition back to the classroom.

- Whenever possible, assign a peer partner to the student with ASD for his Walk and Talk Break. This encourages interaction among students. In addition to academically focused activities, you can use general conversation starters for these breaks with classmates.

Relevant IFSP or IEP Goals

Consider whether or not the following goals might be appropriate for children with ASD who are participating in Walk and Talk Breaks.

- Preschool—Given a verbal prompt, the student will take a break with a partner during three consecutive opportunities.

- Kindergarten—Given a visual prompt, the student will take a break with a partner during three consecutive opportunities.

- First or second grade—Student will articulate a need for a break without problem behaviors during three consecutive opportunities.

Technology Resources to Help Address Behavioral Concerns for Students with ASD

- Practical Autism Resources (http://www .practicalautismresources.com/printables) has several free printable resources, including ABC charts, data forms, and behavior charts, to help address behavior concerns.

- Find a behavior chart that focuses on a student specific goal at Free Printable Behavior Charts (http://www .freeprintablebehaviorcharts.com/homework _charts.htm) or at Kid Pointz (http://www .kidpointz.com/preschool-charts/).

- Building Blox (http://www.buildingblox.net /taskideasandfreebies.html) has many free pdf files of student support materials for children with ASD. Simply download the files, print, and implement.

- Monitor class behavior with ClassDojo (https://www.classdojo.com/), an online positive behavior management system for teachers. Provides students, families, and teachers with feedback on students' behavior via computer or mobile device.

- Positively Autism (http://positivelyautism .weebly.com/freebies-improving-behavior .html) has several resources for shaping the behavior of students with ASD. Explore online tutorials, free printables, and research materials on this website.

- Create social stories that are specific to individual students with the Stories About Me app (http://www.friendshipcircle.org/apps /browse/stories-about-me/). Add photos, text, and audio to produce engaging stories for students.

- The Early Autism Project (http:// earlyautismproject.com/blog/free-aba -materials-for-families/) has compiled several websites that offer resources and materials that you can use with applied behavior analysis (ABA) methods.

- Autism Speaks (https://www.autismspeaks .org/family-services/tool-kits/challenging -behaviors-tool-kit) offers a challenging behavior tool kit. Download sections of the printed resource or the whole text for ideas and suggestions for dealing with challenging behaviors.

Key Terms

antecedent-behavior-consequence chart: A chart that documents what happens before a behavior (the antecedent), the behavior, and what happens after the behavior (the consequence).

applied behavior analysis (ABA): A systematic approach to target a person's behavioral needs based on the principles of positive reinforcement.

behavior function: Describes the reason an individual engages in the behavior (for example, to avoid a task, to earn attention, and so on).

behavior intervention plan: Outlines specific strategies that the team will use to decrease problem behaviors and increase prosocial choices.

behavior type: Describes the type of behavior (for example, aggressive, self-stimulatory, and so on).

replacement behaviors: Prosocial behaviors designed to replace more challenging behaviors. Replacement behaviors must serve the same function as the initial challenging behaviors.

7

Helping to Build Social Relationships with Peers

It's free playtime in Ms. Keller's second-grade classroom. Children are scattered about the room, engaged in several activities. Two girls are playing a board game. Another group of students is playing concentration. Many others are partnered together on computers in the technology center. Jacob is sitting alone at his desk. Ten minutes into playtime, a few boys ask Jacob to join them in racing toy cars. They need one more racer to make the teams even. Jacob ignores the students, flipping aimlessly through an animal magazine at his desk. Ms. Keller looks at the clock. It is time to begin reading. She announces to students that free playtime is over; everyone must clean up their materials. Many students begin to put their toys away. Jacob continues to turn pages in his magazine. Ms. Keller walks over to Jacob. She whispers to him, "Time to clean up, Jacob." Looking down at the magazine, Jacob shows Ms. Keller a photo of a snake. His face lights up immediately. "Look, look a snake! Snakes are cool. They smell with their tongues," Jacob yells. Several students begin to stare at Jacob. "They smell like this," Jacob exclaims again, only this time he begins to thrust his tongue in and out of his mouth. Jacob moves quickly around the room. He places himself close to his classmates as he sticks his tongue close to their faces. Some children complain that Jacob is spitting on them as he moves from student to student, showing them how a snake smells. After several minutes, Ms. Keller is able to persuade Jacob to return to his seat. As she begins to organize students for partner reading, a student complains when she is paired to work with Jacob.

What Are Social Skills?

Very simply stated, social skills allow people to interact with each other. Young students use social skills to communicate and share their thoughts, feelings, and ideas. Yet social skills vary greatly among young students because children develop these abilities at different rates and to different degrees. It is easy to identify students at either end of the social continuum. Some students are social whizzes. They make friends easily, work well with many students, and are sensitive to other children's feelings. Other children are more withdrawn. These children have limited friendships and are often viewed as loners.

Frequently, students with ASD are in this second category. Because it is difficult for them to understand the thoughts and feelings of others, students with ASD struggle to engage well with peers. For example, if a child with ASD likes cell phones and enjoys talking about them, he will assume that cell phones are a shared interest of others. If this child talks about his father's cell phone for show-and-share every week, he will not notice that other children are bored by this topic. Focused on his own thinking, this student will miss the facial cues and body language that express his classmates' thoughts.

Recognizing and empathizing with others' emotions is also challenging for students with ASD. Consider this example: A student with ASD is working at a computer. He is working to reach the final level of a math addition fact game. Meanwhile, another student in the classroom has tripped over the leg of a desk and hit her head. Although this child is sobbing and other children are focused on their hurt classmate, the student with ASD pushes through the crowd of students to show the teacher he has finally reached the final level of the computer game. The student with ASD has failed to recognize that the emotional need of his classmate is of greater significance than his own in this moment.

Another important part of social skill development for young children is learning to understand and regulate their own feelings. Insensitive adults sometimes assume that young children do not experience the same intensity of emotions as adults simply because they cannot always put those feelings into words. However, young children's emotions are felt just as strongly, even though they may be prompted by something that appears inconsequential to an adult. How children express their feelings is significant. For instance, a kindergartener with ASD is angry because another student is sitting next to her friend at lunch. As a result, she grabs the other child's lunch and throws it on the floor. This response is inappropriate because it affects others in a negative way. As shown in this example, many children with ASD need to learn to identify and manage feelings properly in order to interact well with peers.

The Importance of Social Skills

As illustrated through these examples, limited social skills can affect relationships with others. Difficulty interpreting the thoughts and feelings of others can hinder how well students with ASD interact with others. Teachers who do not address these skills with their students with ASD risk isolating them from the classroom community. Because social interaction is such a significant part of the early childhood experience, gaps in social learning can easily impede academic growth as well.

Too often, educators associate social skills with general personality traits. This is a profound mistake. Social skills are not just personal characteristics that are nice to have; instead, these abilities are essential to independent functioning in the outside world. In fact, students with ASD can experience several problems because of delays in social development. In his guide for teachers, parents, and professionals, Martin Kutscher highlighted several negative consequences that students with ASD may struggle with as a direct result of poor social skills:

- **High anxiety and nervousness.** Since students with ASD do not always know how to respond in many social settings, they can become very worried and upset that their reaction will be inappropriate.

- **Reduced self-confidence.** As a result of not knowing what to do or say with peers, students with ASD may begin to believe that they are "stupid" or "dumb."

- **Peer avoidance.** Responses from a child with ASD in social settings can sometimes be perceived as rude or impolite. For example, classmates may not want to be around the child who gives too many details about being sick over the weekend.

- **Social isolation.** Just as peers may avoid the child with limited social skills, students with ASD may begin to isolate themselves from social activities. For many students with ASD, engaging with others socially is difficult work. It may feel easier to simply avoid these situations altogether. Another type of isolation results from language barriers. Slang, sarcasm, or even riddles or jokes can be complicated for students with ASD to interpret and can make them feel like an outsider within a group of peers.

- **Inattentiveness.** Because many students with ASD often find it difficult to relate to the interests or feelings of others, these students may tune out while others are speaking or expressing concerns, yet become quite talkative about an intensely focused interest.

- **Connectedness with things rather than people.** Unlike people, objects do not have expectations for social give-and-take. When it becomes too difficult to interact with

people, students with ASD may substitute things for people to gain a sense of comfort and reliability.

Social Deficits in Children with ASD

Social deficits are one of the characteristics of an ASD diagnosis. Similar to other traits of ASD, social deficits vary from person to person, ranging from significant delays to minor quirks. In a 1979 journal article, Lorna Wing and Judith Gould identified three areas of deficit for children with ASD, which are referred to as the "triad of impairments." These directly influence social development in the following ways:

- **Social interaction.** Deficits in the ability to engage and interact with people. Examples: Difficulty playing and working with others appropriately. Problems making and maintaining friendships.

- **Social imagination.** Deficits in the ability to comprehend alternative viewpoints. Examples: Lack of empathy toward others. Rigid thinking patterns.

- **Social communication.** Deficits in the ability to speak and understand language. Examples: Frequent misunderstandings of social cues, gestures, or body language. Difficulty expressing thoughts and ideas.

Consider the story at the opening of this chapter. Jacob's behaviors illustrate several examples of the triad of impairments. First, social deficits are apparent in Jacob's interaction with his peers. Certainly, Jacob is interested in his classmates and wants to build relationships with them. This is why he tries to share information about how snakes smell with several students. Snakes are apparently interesting to Jacob, and he wants to share this interest with his friends. Unfortunately, Jacob has not been taught an appropriate way to share that information. His behaviors of invading students' personal space, sticking his tongue out at them, and possibly spitting on them are not effective ways to interact socially with his peers.

Next, Jacob shows deficits in his social imagination. Although the teacher has announced the end of free playtime, Jacob has failed to acknowledge Ms. Keller's plans to continue with the class schedule. Although free playtime is over, Jacob continues to focus on his own routine. Similarly, he does not consider that others may not be interested in snakes or how they use their sense of smell. Even when his classmates show signs of being bothered, Jacob continues to talk about snakes. Jacob's rigidity in thinking has made it difficult to consider how either his teacher or his classmates might be feeling.

Last, this story highlights how Jacob's social deficits are compounded by some communication needs. Think about how Jacob might have negotiated his interaction with his classmates better had he described his behavior first—"Hi guys! Did you know that snakes smell with their tongues? That's why they move them in and out like this" (*showing movement*). This simple introduction completely changes the context of Jacob's behavior, making it more socially acceptable.

Additionally, language does more than give meaning to actions. It is a key component of relationship building. At a young age, children learn to use communication as a social resource. Language helps students identify common interests, understand feelings, and solve problems. As students engage in these processes, they gain experience interacting with others, which increases their social aptitude. The combination of language and social delays that students with ASD face, however, can hinder their social progress tremendously.

Yet just because gaining social skills is difficult does not mean it is impossible. A student with ASD who engages in an activity by herself does not necessarily prefer to play alone. In fact, many students with ASD want to be included with their peers even though connecting socially with others may feel awkward to them. It is the teacher's job to help students with ASD navigate social situations with peers and gain skills that will help them fit in at school.

The "Hidden Curriculum"

In 1968, Phillip Jackson assigned the term hidden curriculum to the social rules that are taught in schools. In his observations of school classrooms, Jackson found that schools taught students not only academic subjects, but also expectations for behaviors. However, unlike reading or mathematics, these skills were not explicitly taught, but rather taught through day-to-day school experiences. In his research, Jackson found that students who were successful in school did so by learning ways to get along with other people (classmates) and to please authority figures (teachers).

Most typically developing children learn these implicit social skills through observation. They watch others and then try to replicate the behavior in new situations. Students with ASD, conversely, must be taught explicitly how to interact with others. Teachers must take the time to explain social tasks step by step so that students with ASD can understand how and when to use skills appropriately in the natural environment. However, this process is hugely complex, because it requires that teachers anticipate student responses and develop individual plans for addressing social needs.

Typically, students with ASD do not learn social skills implicitly. These students must learn ways to interact with others through the explicit teaching of steps. Review the steps educators could use to teach a student how to get the teacher's attention, as shown in figure 7.1, then write practice writing steps for another school social skill (for example, greeting a friend, introducing yourself, or listening to others).

Figure 7.1   Teaching Social Skills from the Hidden Curricuum

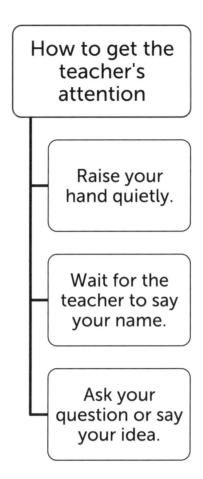

Building Social Skills in Students with ASD

School is one of the best places for students with ASD to learn and practice social skills. Classrooms offer natural settings for peer inter-action as well as multiple student groups with which to rehearse skills. If teachers plan care-fully, it is possible to integrate social skills training into daily school activities. Additionally, the routine of school gives students with ASD an opportunity to generalize skills over time. The following are recommendations for ways to teach social skills in early childhood classrooms:

- **Practice body language and facial expressions.** People say a great deal without using words. Consequently, learning to read facial and body cues can help students with ASD better understand peer responses. Use books and magazines to teach students with ASD how various emotions are portrayed by people's faces and bodies. Encourage students to draw, write, or talk about their own feelings. Have them make collages of faces that depict emotions—first, the obvious ones (such as sad, mad, and glad), and then more subtle ones (such as worried, confused, and afraid).

- **Use peers.** Peers are very valuable resources for students with ASD learning social skills. Encourage students to model appropriate behaviors. Point out the use of appropriate social skills in action.

- **Teach play skills.** In early childhood classrooms, many social skills are taught through play activities. Design structured play centers that require students with ASD to use appropriate play skills, such as sharing and cooperating with others.

- **Show the importance of taking turns.** Taking turns is a foundational conversation skill. However, it can be difficult for some students to understand the importance of turn-taking. Use games to showcase how turn-taking works. Have student partners pass a prop (a small toy or ball) between each other to show visually how turn-taking occurs in conversation.

- **Role-play social situations.** Students with ASD can become anxious when they do not understand how to respond or behave in a situation. Use role-playing to allow students to practice social skills under specific circumstances.

- **Show students ways to manage their own feelings.** Although social skills focus on getting along with others, they also require students to manage their own emotions. Teach students effective ways to manage their feelings so that problem behaviors do not hinder relationship building.

- **Discuss ways to show respect.** Talk about respect with all students. List examples of ways they can show respect (for example, by listening while others speak, accepting differences, and helping others). Teach students how to respond appropriately when their feelings are hurt.

- **Teach students to "self-talk."** Encourage students to think through social situations before they act. Teach social skills as a series of steps and show students how to talk themselves through each step in their head as they interact with others.

- **Enact anti-bullying procedures.** Students who struggle to understand and get along with others can become the targets of bullying behavior. Students with ASD, especially, are at risk for being targeted by individuals who do not understand how ASD affects social interaction. Help students include others who feel left out. Intervene when students are being teased or hurt.

- **Effective social skills are extremely valuable throughout life.** Children who interact well with others are more likely to have more friendships, greater self-confidence, and better problem-solving skills. Students with ASD can have these social advantages when they are taught to use social skills explicitly and given frequent opportunities to practice in a natural setting. The following strategies are ways to teach social skills to young students with ASD.

Strategies to Build Social Skills in Students with ASD

Emotional Charades

Materials
Index cards
Marker
Bag or box for cards

Why Use This Strategy?
Many students with ASD find it challenging to read the emotions of others and interpret their feelings. As a result, students with ASD may behave in ways that are socially awkward.

Emotional Charades is a fun way for students to practice identifying different emotions. This game encourages students with ASD to focus on facial cues to recognize what others are feeling. In addition, this strategy can help students better recognize and express their own feelings.

How Does This Strategy Work?

- Determine a list of common emotions (for example, happy, sad, angry, surprised, silly, lonely, bored, frustrated, disappointed, and tired).

- Write the feelings on small cards and place them in a box or bag.

- Have a student select a card. Read the card for the student, or ask her to read it aloud. Then, have the student attempt to act out the emotion on the card.

- Ask the remaining students to try to guess the emotion that the student is portraying. The student who guesses the emotion correctly continues the game by choosing a card.

Teacher Tips

- Discuss the emotions listed on the game cards prior to beginning the game. Practice reading the emotions of individuals in books or magazines first.

- Before play begins, model how some of the emotions could be expressed. Show how some emotions are communicated through body language.

- After each emotion is guessed correctly, discuss various situations when a student might be feeling that emotion. Identify appropriate peer responses to these situations as a follow-up activity.

- When students become skilled at acting out and identifying emotions, make the game more challenging. Provide students with a situation and have them show an appropriate emotional response. (For example, "Your classmate invited you to her birthday party." *happy, excited* or "The teacher said recess is over." *sad, frustrated*).

Relevant IFSP or IEP Goals

Consider whether or not the following goals might be appropriate for children with ASD who are participating in Emotional Charades.

- Preschool—Using facial cues, the student will correctly identify the happy emotion expressed in adults or peers in four out of five opportunities.

- Kindergarten—Using facial cues, the student will correctly distinguish between happy and sad emotions expressed in adults or peers in four out of five opportunities.

- First or second grade—Using facial cues, the student will correctly identify five different emotions expressed in adults or peers in four out of five opportunities.

Play Pals
Why Use This Strategy?

Less-structured activities can be very stressful for students with ASD. Lunch and recess, for instance, are highly unpredictable and difficult for many students to navigate. This is why so many children with ASD are withdrawn in these types of settings.

Play Pals connects students with ASD with their typically developing peers during free periods. Play Pals uses peers to model appropriate social interaction to help students with ASD engage in play activities.

How Does This Strategy Work?

- Select students to act as play pals. These students should be friendly and outgoing, but also patient and helpful.

- Pair play pals with students with ASD.

- During free playtime or recess, have play pals partner with students with ASD. Play pals should encourage students with ASD to engage in play activities or conversation. See the suggested activities that follow.

- Monitor play pals and their partners, and offer support and guidance as needed.

Suggested Interactive Activities

- *Playing catch*
- *Jumping rope*
- *Soccer drills*
- *Kickball*
- *Board games*

Suggested Parallel-Play Activities

- *Swinging*
- *Drawing with sidewalk chalk*
- *Blowing bubbles*
- *Modeling with clay*
- *Building with blocks*

Teacher Tips

- Help play pals understand their role. Give them suggestions of how to engage their partners in play. Have games and activities available that both students enjoy.

- Whenever possible, match play pals with students who have similar interests.

- Rotate play pals often. Encouraging students with ASD to engage socially is hard work. Never force students to be play pals.

- Some students may need multiple play pals. Students can play together as a group or take turns partnering with the student with ASD in five- to seven-minute intervals.

Relevant IFSP or IEP Goals

Consider whether or not the following goals might be appropriate for children with ASD who are participating in Play Pals activities.

- Preschool—When guided by a peer, the student will engage in social play for at least three minutes for three consecutive days.

- Kindergarten—When guided by a peer, the student will engage in social play for at least five minutes for three consecutive days.

- First or second grade—When guided by a peer, the student will engage in social play for at least ten minutes for three consecutive days.

Meet and Greet

Materials
Index cards
Marker

Why Use This Strategy?

Greetings are very simple forms of conversation. When children with ASD learn to greet others, they begin to acknowledge others in the world around them. Through this basic interaction, children learn to communicate and engage with people.

Meet and Greets are a fun way to teach young students common greetings. As part of a daily class meeting, Meet and Greets give students an opportunity to build relationships with peers. Further, this strategy provides guided practice of socialization skills that can be generalized to people and places beyond the classroom.

How Does This Strategy Work?

- Have students meet in a common area in the classroom. This can be a carpeted area, reading center, or another designated area. All students should be able to sit comfortably in the area.

- During Meet and Greet time, have each student greet and respond to a partner using three steps:

1. The students use a greeting (for example, "Good Morning, Cameron," or "Hello, Mina") and call the classmate by name.

2. Students can choose to wave, high-five, fist bump, or shake hands with their classmates.

3. Students ask their partner the daily question. A list of sample daily questions follows.

- After students have completed all three steps, they can begin the process again with another partner.

Teacher Tips

- Consider having a sign or signal to begin and end the meet and greet time. This will help ease transitioning. A hand signal or clap pattern works well.

- Model this activity for the class frequently. Use a student partner to show how to greet and respond to questions appropriately.

- Teach students to wait for a response before moving to the next step in the greeting. For instance, if a student waves to his partner, he should wait for a reciprocal wave before moving to the next step.

- Allow students to write daily questions they would like to answer. Write daily questions on small cards and place them in a box or bag. You can use a similar procedure for the other steps in the greeting pattern. Allow a student helper to choose which greeting ("hello," "good morning," "howdy," and so on) and body motion (wave, handshake, high five, and so on) to use.

Relevant IFSP or IEP Goals

Consider whether or not the following goals might be appropriate for children with ASD who are participating in Meet and Greet activities.

- Preschool—Given a verbal prompt, the student will greet at least three teachers over five consecutive school days.

- Kindergarten—Given a visual prompt, the student will greet at least three teachers over five consecutive school days.

- First or second grade—Student will initiate a greeting to at least three teachers independently over five consecutive school days.

Sample Daily Questions

- *What did you do last night?*
- *What are you doing this weekend?*
- *How do you feel?*
- *What will you do at school today?*
- *What did you bring for lunch?*
- *What are you doing after school today?*
- *Did you finish your homework?*
- *What is your favorite toy (or color or food)?*
- *Do you have any animals at home? What kind?*

The Compliment Kid Strategy
Why Use This Strategy?

Complimenting others is an important social skill. Through compliments, students can share opinions in a way that is socially acceptable. However, students with ASD must be taught how to give compliments appropriately.

The Compliment Kid strategy focuses on the process of giving and accepting compliments. In this activity, students with ASD can practice stating compliments that are specific and meaningful.

How Does This Strategy Work?

- Select the compliment kid of the day. Choose students alphabetically, randomly, or as a special reward.

- Ask the compliment kid to stand in front of the class or at his desk.

- Select three to five students from the class to share compliments about the compliment kid.

- Initially, some students may need support with giving compliments. Create a help board with compliment starters to assist students. A list of help-board compliment starters follows.

- After each compliment, prompt the compliment kid to accept the compliment by saying words of appreciation ("Thank you," "That was kind," "I appreciate that," and so on).

- Have the compliment kid return to his seat. If time permits, select another compliment kid and repeat the process.

Teacher Tips

- If a student feels uncomfortable being complimented in front of the class, ask students to write or dictate their compliments to a teacher.

- When students become comfortable with this strategy, add a challenge by requiring compliments to fit a specific theme. For example, students can give compliments about outside appearances (clothing, jewelry, hair), inside qualities (kindhearted, friendly, helpful), or performance (good at math, awesome soccer player, neat drawer).

- Students with ASD may need more direct instruction with giving compliments. Consider using this in a small group or individually with the student before integrating it into a daily whole-group routine. Have students use photographs of school personnel or family members to practice giving compliments.

- Consider making the compliments more tangible by having children draw or write something kind that someone else did for them and creating a thank-you card.

Help-Board Compliment Starters

- *I really like your _____.*
- *You're really good at _____.*
- *You have the best _____.*
- *I like the way you _____.*
- *You're _____ because _____.*

Relevant IFSP or IEP Goals

Consider whether or not the following goals might be appropriate for children with ASD who are participating in Compliment Kid activities.

- Preschool—Given a compliment by an adult or peer, the student will thank the individual with verbal prompting.

- Kindergarten—Given a compliment by an adult or peer, the student will thank the individual without prompting.

- First or second grade—With either a visual or verbal prompt, the student will give at least one appropriate compliment to a peer each day for three consecutive school days.

Disappointment Schedule
Materials
Card stock

Marker

Images of coping activities (cut from magazines or drawn)

Glue or tape

Why Use This Strategy?

It is difficult for many young students to cope with disappointment. However, students with ASD, in particular, struggle with coping with the anxiety and frustration that come with not getting their own way. When these feelings are managed improperly, social interaction is deeply compromised.

Disappointment schedules help students with ASD explore prosocial ways to deal with disappointment. Perhaps, even more importantly, this strategy teaches students with ASD to solve their own stressful situations.

How Does This Strategy Work?

- Organize a list of activities with the student with ASD that could help the child manage disappointment. It is important to make the child a part of this process because she will know best what she needs to cope with her feelings. See the list of suggested activities for coping with disappointment that follows.

- Create a list on card stock with three to five activities. Pair activities with pictures attached to the paper so that the student can easily make a selection. You can laminate the schedule if you like.

- When the student feels disappointed, have her take out her disappointment schedule and begin the first activity. Assist the student as needed.

- After the child completes the activity, ask the student how she feels. If the child has recovered from her disappointment, she is encouraged to rejoin the group. If the child is still upset, have her move to the next activity on the schedule.

Teacher Tips

- Assign an area of the classroom as a cool-down space. Have students with ASD store their disappointment schedules there and use the space for their calming activities.

Suggested Activities for Coping with Disappointment

- *A five-minute rest*
- *Relaxing deep breathing*
- *Stroking a stuffed animal or class pet*
- *Looking at a picture book*
- *Softly singing a calm song*
- *Stretching*
- *Talking with a trusted peer or adult*
- *Playing with a miniature toy*

- Encourage students to recognize signs of disappointment and frustration in themselves. Praise students when they manage their disappointments effectively.

Relevant IFSP or IEP Goals

Consider whether or not the following goals might be appropriate for children with ASD who are participating in Disappointment Schedule activities.

- Preschool—Given verbal and visual prompts, the student will manage feelings of disappointment without incident (yelling, crying, hitting, and so on) in three out of five opportunities.

- Kindergarten—Given visual prompts, the student will manage feelings of disappointment without incident (yelling, crying, hitting, and so on) in three out of five opportunities.

- First or second grade—Without prompting, the student will manage feelings of disappointment without incident (yelling, crying, hitting, and so on) in three out of five opportunities.

Social Cue Match: A Small-Group Activity

Materials

Paper
Pictures from magazines or photos
Glue or tape

Why Use This Strategy?

People use their faces and bodies to send signals all the time. Some signs, such as tears or smiles, are easy to understand but other cues can be difficult to interpret. In these situations, students must use social context to determine meaning. Because of communication deficits, however, many young students with ASD struggle with reading social situations properly.

Social Cue Match provides practice with two important social skills. First, students must analyze social situations common to the classroom environment. Second, students must distinguish the facial cues and body language of individuals to match the social context with the appropriate visual response.

How Does This Strategy Work?

- Place an array of three to five photographs of people depicting various emotional states in front of the student. The photographs can be photographs you take of students role-playing different emotions or photographs you cut from magazines.

- Read a short story that describes a problem or significant event. A list of sample social cue match stories follows.

- After listening to the story, have the student determine which of the photographs would best illustrate the body language and facial expressions of the main character of the story.

- If the student has selected an appropriate photograph, the game should continue with a new story. If the student's selection is incorrect, reread the story and prompt the student to select a different photograph.

Sample Social Cue Match Stories

- **Playing games.** *George likes to play Space Raiders on the computer. He has been trying very hard to make it to level 3 on the game. Every time he is at the end of the level he makes a mistake. Which picture shows how George feels?*

- **Going to school.** *Heather is on her way to school. She fell getting off the bus and tore her pants. Her homework fell in a big puddle, and now she is late to class. Which picture shows how Heather feels?*

- **Celebrating a birthday.** *Today is April's birthday. When she walks into the kitchen, her father has cupcakes and ice cream waiting for her. There is a brand new purple bike with a bow waiting for her outside. Which picture shows how April feels?*

- **Talking about the weekend.** *Ryan went to a baseball game this weekend. He had fun with his family. He tells Joey about it at lunch. Ryan talks the whole time about his trip to the baseball game. Joey never gets to talk about his weekend. Which picture shows how Joey feels?*

Teacher Tips

- Encourage students to explain why they matched a particular photograph with a story. Question them about specific social cues (facial cues and body language) represented in the photograph.

- As students improve their skills with this activity, ask them to describe situations from their own experiences that match the emotions in particular photographs.

- Provide support for students who struggle with matching stories to appropriate photographs. Check for understanding after each step. For instance, after reading the story, ask the student how the main character feels. Then, ask the student to point to a photograph that shows the emotion.

Relevant IFSP or IEP Goals

Consider whether or not the following goals might be appropriate for children with ASD who are participating in Social Cue Match activities.

- Preschool—Student will correctly identify the happy emotion depicted in photographs from an array of three photographs in four out of five opportunities.

- Kindergarten—Student will sort ten examples of happy and sad as depicted in photographs in four out of five opportunities.

- First or second grade—Given an array of three photographs, the student will select the photograph that best illustrates the social situation read aloud to him in four out of five opportunities over three consecutive days.

The Polite or Pushy Strategy

Materials

Picture book about politeness

Why Use This Strategy?

Different social settings have different expectations of behavior. By observing others and studying the social environment, children learn to determine acceptable behavior for specific times and places. For children with ASD, reading these cues does not come easily, and as a result, these students can benefit from direct instruction in this skill.

Polite or Pushy allows students to think about two contrasting responses to a social setting, one polite and the other impolite. With the support of the teacher and peers, students with ASD can carefully review the social situation and decide which response is most appropriate.

How Does This Strategy Work?

- Introduce the difference between polite and pushy with a picture book. Try, for example, Ezra Jack Keats's *Kitten for a Day,* which has limited text. A puppy tries to do everything that the kittens do with humorous, slapstick results. You can view a video on YouTube (https://www.youtube.com/watch?v=BQeK22KiUzc).

- Discuss the words *polite* and *pushy* with the class. For example, "Students who are polite use manners. Students who are pushy try to get attention by being loud, rude, and disrespectful. Most people prefer to be around others who make polite rather than pushy choices."

- Give students a social situation and describe two different responses. One response should be polite while the other is pushy. See the sample social situation stories and responses that follow.

- After you describe each response, ask students to indicate whether the response could be described as polite or pushy. Students will signal with either a thumbs-up (polite) or thumbs-down (pushy).

- Once the majority of students agree on the polite response, have students discuss why the response is appropriate for the social situation.

Teacher Tips

- As students get better at identifying the polite response, encourage them to role-play each social situation. Allow students to brainstorm their own responses to each scenario.

Sample Social Situation Story 1

Our school is having a fire drill. Classes are lined up outside on the playground. Mr. Fernandez, the school principal, is watching to see that all of the classes exit the school safely. What should you do?

Response 1
You begin to talk loudly to your friends. You run around the playground and play on the swings.

Response 2
You stand quietly. When it is time to return to class, you walk in a line back to the classroom.

Sample Social Situation Story 2

Your classmate drew a picture of her family. She used only red to color her drawing. You think your picture is better. What do you do?

Response 1
You listen while your friend describes her picture. You tell her that you like red too.

Response 2
You yell, "That's ugly!" and tell your friend that you don't like her picture.

Sample Social Situation Story 3

It is time for art class. The teacher asks all of the students to line up. Yesterday, you were first in line, but today you are third in line. You like being first. What should you do?

Response 1
You push ahead of the other students. You cry and scream until the teacher lets you be first in line.

Response 2
You stand quietly in your space in line. You ask if you can be first tomorrow.

- Whenever possible, use situations common to classroom experiences. This will allow students to generalize skills more readily.

- Pair this activity with the response card strategy described in Chapter 5. In this variation, have students use cards with happy or sad faces to indicate whether the response is polite or pushy.

Relevant IFSP or IEP Goals
Consider whether or not the following goals might be appropriate for children with ASD who are participating in Polite or Pushy activities.

- Preschool—Given a social situation, the student will select an appropriate response from two alternatives in three out of four opportunities over five consecutive days.

- Kindergarten—Given a social situation, the student will draw an appropriate response in two out of three opportunities.

- First or second grade—Student will describe an appropriate response to a given social situation in three out of four opportunities over five consecutive days.

Technology Resources for Building Social Skills in Students with ASD

- Autism Teaching Strategies (http://autismteachingstrategies.com/free-social-skills-downloads-2) offers several practical activities and games to teach social skills to students with ASD. Printable resources for students are also available.

- Class activities that focus on specific social skills, like sharing and taking turns, are presented at LoveToKnow (http://autism.lovetoknow.com/Preschool_Activities_for_Autistic_Children). Education.com (http://www.education.com/magazine/article/10-activities-children-autism/) offers ten fun ways to engage children with ASD in social learning.

- Students can learn how their peers with ASD think and learn in this child-friendly video presented by Autism Atlas (https://www.youtube.com/watch?feature=player_embedded&v=wES6ZeoDaUs).

- Sandbox Learning (http://www.sandbox-learning.com/RunScript.asp?page=37&ap=view_products.asp&p=ASP\~PgDefault.asp) offers social skill storybooks and activity cards. Teachers can customize both the text and pictures of the books to match students' likes and dislikes. When educators register with the website, they can earn a free storybook.

- Autism Emotion (https://itunes.apple.com/us/app/autism-emotion/id550027186?mt=8) provides free, colorful illustrations to help students distinguish between various emotions.

- Incorporate picture books into social skills learning. Vanderbilt University (http://csefel.vanderbilt.edu/documents/booklist.pdf) has compiled an extensive list of children's books that address emotions. You can use the illustrations to help students identify feelings.

- Visit JumpStart (http://www.jumpstart.com/parents/worksheets/social-skills-worksheets) for several printable worksheets for leading social skills lessons in preschool through third grade classrooms.

- Use comic strips to teach social skills in a fun and interactive way. At MakeBeliefsComix (http://www.makebeliefscomix.com/Comix/), teachers can make comic strips to showcase how to engage appropriately in social interactions.

Key Terms

hidden curriculum: Implicitly taught social rules that focus on ways to get along with other people and to please authority figures.

social skills: Abilities that help children interact with each other successfully.

triad of impairments: Deficits in social communication, social imagination, and social interaction that occur in the development of students with ASD.

8 Building Partnerships with Families

Jackson is beginning kindergarten. Although his parents are excited about his new school, Jackson is worried and upset about leaving the preschool he has attended for the last two years. The first week of school, Jackson cries each day when his mother leaves him and asks the teacher repeatedly when school will be over. One month later, Jackson's parents suggest that Jackson's teacher use a visual schedule to help him organize his day. While Jackson was in preschool and during home therapy, Jackson's parents saw how a visual schedule helped him focus on activities. Nonetheless, the teacher politely disregards the suggestion, relying on her own professional teaching experience. As months pass, Jackson has made limited progress in class. Although he had demonstrated many strong academic skills in preschool, Jackson struggles to complete assignments in kindergarten. After several weeks of problem behaviors, the team stumbles upon a significant realization—that Jackson feels anxious and overwhelmed throughout the school day. Six months into the kindergarten school year, Jackson's support team introduces a visual schedule to his inclusion plan.

Understanding Parent Roles

As this story illustrates, ignoring family insight can delay progress for students with ASD. While teacher training and classroom experience are helpful, no amount of professional development can prepare teachers for the unique manifestations of pervasive developmental disorders in individual children. Parents and families know their child's characteristics in ways that educators cannot. In day-to-day activities, many families provide support to help their children with ASD navigate the world around them. This is why parent expertise is so valuable. However, building partnerships with parents takes time and effort.

So why is it such a challenge for professionals and parents of children with ASD to collaborate? Parents and teachers have differing perspectives. According to Patricia Sheehey and Patrick Sheehey in their journal article about family-teacher collaboration, educators ground their decision-making on their training and experience, and parents tend to make choices for their children based on personal experience. Neither method is better than the other. In fact, both approaches are necessary to support children with ASD. It is the job of the early childhood educator to adopt this mind-set and to find ways to partner with families to support student progress.

While building relationships with families, teachers should remember that not every parent wants to participate in his child's education in the same way. Families will respond to teacher input differently, and sometimes, in multiple ways at once. Teachers must realize that some parents' knowledge of ASD and how it manifests in their children exceeds their own understanding. Accordingly, teachers should broaden their idea of parent involvement to include efforts beyond academic support. A parent who is willing to offer insight on how to help her son make friends is just as influential as the parent who helps her daughter study spelling words. While advocating for their child, families often assume one or more of three very important roles: protector, evaluator, and coteacher. To maximize student potential, teachers must learn to recognize and value each of these roles, which are explained briefly in table 8.1.

Parents as Protectors

When working with learners with ASD and their families, educators must always be mindful of the extraordinary value these children hold for their families. Despite their child's disability, parents of students with ASD care very deeply for their children and have goals, hopes, and dreams for them. They want their children to be successful and lead productive, happy lives. This is why parents of children with ASD need teachers to include them in the decision-making that will help to realize these goals.

As protectors, parents need to see evidence that teachers are implementing strategies to help their children succeed. These families want

Table 8.1 Roles of Parents of Children with ASD

Family Member Role	Efforts to Support Families
Protector	• Family members want to know that their child feels safe and included.
	• Families want to see effective interventions implemented in school.
Evaluator	• Family members want to be included in decision-making about their child's education.
	• Families want their expertise as parents recognized and valued.
Coteacher	• Teachers strive to be aware of goals for the student at home.
	• Teachers and family members can work to support one another's efforts with the child.

regular communication that shows progress toward students' academic, social, and behavioral goals. Further, parents in the role of protector need to know that their child feels safe and included in school. Consider a parent who informs his child's teacher that his child is being teased on the bus. The teacher can respond by offering assistance or by ignoring the problem. The teacher who intervenes in efforts to stop the bullying gains the trust and support of the family. Conversely, the teacher who disregards the parent's concern causes irreversible damage to her relationship with the family.

Parents as Evaluators

One of the best advantages of school-home partnerships is that each party offers a critical awareness that the other lacks. While parents know the personal strengths and weaknesses of their children, school professionals provide experience, training, and objectivity. With parents and professionals providing unique expertise, collaboration among these groups is crucial to evaluating the effectiveness of student programming and interventions.

It can be difficult for teachers to escape the tendency to compare one child to another and find a child lacking or deficient in some way. Although teachers understand that every child is unique and learns differently, students who don't meet teacher expectations easily are often regarded as less capable than others. This creates a rift between home and school. Most parents see their children as intelligent and skillful, but school personnel sometimes shake that belief system.

When parents act as evaluators, they provide insight into how their child's needs are being met within the classroom. These parents want to be included in decision-making about their child's education. Most importantly, in this role parents want to know that their voice is being heard and their recommendations are being implemented in the classroom. Parent evaluators want to be recognized as equals with school professionals in planning for their child's educational goals.

In the opening story of this chapter, Jackson's parents are acting as evaluators. Based on past experiences, the family knows that Jackson will benefit from a visual schedule. When they shared this insight with school staff, they expected the support team to be receptive to the idea. Instead, their perspective was ignored. This type of response from the school can have a negative effect on relationships with parents of students with ASD.

Parents as Coteachers

Classroom teachers cannot educate a child with ASD independently. Teachers and parents each have roles in the learning and development of students. Making an effort to include parents of children with ASD in educational planning helps to build mutual respect and understanding among teachers and parents. Truly, these are the building blocks of lasting student achievement.

The traditional view of family involvement is of parents supporting the teacher's efforts— particularly with academic learning tasks. Yet for a variety of reasons, parents may not have the inclination, time, or confidence to do this. Often, teachers express frustration when they send something home—such as vocabulary flash cards—and parents do not practice the task with students as requested. The parent as coteacher model, however, recognizes that teachers can support the work of parents with their children.

When teachers are aware of the goals families have for their children in the home setting, they can reinforce those expectations at school through instruction and practice. For instance, if the family wants the student to build functional independence, educators can incorporate school-appropriate self-help skills into the child's daily instruction. Activities such as tying shoes, washing hands, or purchasing a school lunch can reinforce home goals in the school setting.

Providing Support to Families

To assist parents in assuming their advocacy roles, educators must offer families support. Throughout their experience raising a child with ASD, parents will need different types and levels of support. Educators can help by being aware of the needs of these families and matching them with support that is both effective and adequate. R. A. McWilliam and Stacy Scott suggested in their journal article about early intervention that families of children with special needs require three types of support: informational, material, and emotional.

Informational support helps families better understand their child's disability and its effects on development. Websites, pamphlets, and school conferences can provide informational support to families.

Material support focuses on delivering resources to the family so that basic needs can be met. Assisting a family in completing an application for free and reduced lunch is one example of how a teacher might offer material support.

Finally, emotional support reinforces the relationship between the parent and the child by caring for the mental well-being of the family. One of the best ways teachers can offer emotional support is through a sense of empathy.

Building Empathy

The scenario that follows provides some insight into issues that might arise for families of children with ASD.

Ava just completed kindergarten, and she was sharing her yearbook with a family member at a summer cookout. They sat on the porch swing together while Ava chatted about her friends. Then, Ava turned the conversation to "kids who get in trouble all of the time." Ava pointed out several "bad" kids and described their behavior, including "he knocked me down on the playground," and "she talked back to the teacher and got sent to the principal's office." She turned to another child's photo and said, "He's bad . . . ," but then shook her head vigorously and corrected herself with, "No, that's not right. He has *special needs.*"

Imagine if you were this child's parent and overheard this comment about your son. Even though Ava was more understanding than many children her age, it would be hurtful nonetheless.

Being a parent is difficult, but raising a child with ASD is especially challenging. Many skills that typically developing students learn through their natural environment must be taught explicitly to children with ASD. Further, delays in communication can make this process long and complex. Many skills must be taught and retaught to make minimal progress. Even then, it can take some children with ASD years to accomplish simple tasks independently, and retention of these skills is never guaranteed.

Further, many stages of development are significantly more challenging when paired with ASD. Very often, there are gaps between biological and developmental ages for these youths. For example, although many young children struggle with separation anxiety, these feelings may be more intense or persist beyond the preschool years for students with ASD because of uneven development. For children with ASD, separation from loved ones in the school setting can create confusion and frustration, making self-regulation difficult. It is not unusual for some students with ASD to regress in skills when they are placed in new environments.

All of these challenges create stress for parents of children with ASD. All of the common parental worries about children fitting in, adjusting to school life, and making academic progress are intensified for parents of children with ASD. Nonetheless, it is important that families remain positive and hopeful about the future. Teachers should support parent advocacy by providing empathy. This does not mean that teachers feel sorry for families with children with ASD; there are many joys in raising a child with ASD. Instead, teachers should try to understand the perspective of the parent and share in these feelings. Parents should not feel alone as they guide their child with ASD through school experiences. Table 8.2 explains three ways that teachers can show empathy in interactions with parents of children with ASD.

Soliciting Parent Insight

Teachers have many resources that they can use to support students' learning. Students' interests, professional training, and specialized knowledge are some of the tools teachers use to meet students' needs. Yet when they have gaps in their understanding and skills, teachers frequently resort to that lowest form of learning—trial and error—to find what works for students. It's easy to see the problem with this approach; few parents are willing to experiment with their children's education and take the chance that the child will fail as a result.

Parents, like teachers, have resources that can support students' learning. Families are often very aware of their child's likes and dislikes. This information can be very helpful to

teachers. If the teacher knows that unfamiliar clothing bothers her student with ASD, the teacher would be less likely to insist that the child wear an oversized T-shirt to paint at the art center. Recognizing the child's aversion to unfamiliar clothing could prevent a meltdown in the classroom.

Families also have very specific knowledge on how to best help their child manage day-to-day activities. For example, parents of children with ASD know how to prepare their children to eat at a restaurant, transition from play activities, or shop at a grocery store. These skills come from daily interaction with their children in different settings. The practical value of these experiences in school is endless.

Because of their differing perspectives and expertise, parents and teachers should partner to support students with ASD. Many of the strategies families practice with students at home are also useful at school. Consider how a parent must manage her child's behaviors at the grocery store. She must make sure that her daughter keeps her hands to herself, walks appropriately throughout the store, and waits patiently in line. Many of these skills are also necessary at school. Asking for parents' insight can help teachers solve problems more efficiently.

However, many families have had prior experiences with schools—perhaps during their own childhoods—that were disappointing. This baggage from previous school experiences can inhibit families' ability to collaborate with educators because the bond of trust has been damaged. Other families may

Table 8.2 Ways to Show Empathy to Parents of Students with ASD

Show Interest in Conversations	Listen without Judgment	Show Support
• Maintain eye contact • Ask questions • Focus on what is said, not what to say next	• Consider the parents' perspectives • Ask families to explain their feelings and reasoning • Avoid rushing to a solution	• Ask how to help • Highlight positive qualities of the child or the family support system

define their roles as providing food, shelter, clothing, and emotional support to their child while all of the formal learning is the responsibility of the professional educator. Still other families may want to work with the school but feel ill-equipped to participate in a conversation with someone who has more education and is an authority figure. Consequently, it is left to the teacher to create working relationships with families. Building these partnerships takes time, trust, and mutual respect. Teachers should not give parents the impression that they are overwhelmed by a child's needs; asking for parent insight should not be a cry for help. Instead, teachers should collaborate with parents to support and evaluate interventions already in place.

Communicating with Families

Teachers of children with ASD may encounter a variety of communication challenges, such as the following scenario.

Interacting with peers was challenging for Trevor, but today was particularly difficult. Just after recess, he grabbed Christopher's glasses from his face and threw them across the classroom. When his teacher, Mr. Anderson, asked him to defend his actions, Trevor simply stared at the ground and mumbled something to himself. Mr. Anderson sighed heavily. He was now faced with the difficult task of discussing the incident with Trevor's family. Mr. Anderson did not know how he could explain behavior that even Trevor could not rationalize.

Difficult conversations like the one Mr. Anderson is planning are part of establishing open communication with families. Open communication is important because it allows families and educators to interact in ways that facilitate effective decision-making. Because children with ASD have communication delays, relying on students to carry information between school and home is often ineffective.

Instead, teachers will have to explore other ways to build open communication with families of students with ASD.

There are several methods of communication that are available to teachers. Each has its own benefits and shortcomings. Teachers may wish to consider a combination of communication means to reach parents. However, parents may have a preferred method of communication based on their work schedules, resources, or availability. Before the school year begins, teachers can be proactive in discussing appropriate communication methods for families of students with ASD.

Telephone Calls

A phone call is one way to get immediate feedback from families. Teachers can contact parents to inform them of concerns or celebrations as they occur in the classroom. In some cases, it may even be possible for students themselves to share information with their families. When the phone call is a positive contact, hearing it in the student's voice can be especially memorable for families. However, contacting families via phone is not always possible. In many families, both parents work outside the home. Some families may be unavailable to take personal calls during the day. In addition, coordinating schedules after the school day can be difficult for teachers.

Email

Email may be a more convenient way for teachers to communicate with some parents. Because many people can now access email on phones, tablets, and other mobile devices, messages can often provide prompt responses from families. Further, email is both time- and date-stamped, making it an excellent form of documentation. Unfortunately, not every family has access to technology. Another concern is that the tone of email messages can be interpreted in many ways. Words that are meant to convey concern can very easily be misunderstood, possibly damaging relationships between the home and school.

Printed Notes

Paper notes are still used frequently in many contemporary classrooms. Printed records allow teachers to share information and document concerns. Unlike email, paper notes are equally accessible to all families, regardless of their technical knowledge or resources. Yet printed notes do not usually allow for a rapid response. Because the teacher must rely on the student to deliver the note home, it is difficult to guarantee that families will receive the note or will answer quickly.

Determining an efficient way to communicate with parents of students with ASD will take time and planning. However, open communication with families promotes ongoing support and progress for students. The checklist that follows will help you see the strengths and needs in your current home communication plan.

Encouraging Parent Involvement

Communication alone cannot support student growth. Parent involvement is important too. By involving families in students' learning, students with ASD gain additional practice of skills. In addition, families grow in their abilities to support their child's learning. When families observe learning in the classroom, volunteer for school events, or simply assist with homework assignments, they better understand how their child with ASD learns and how they can reinforce skills in the home setting. Parent involvement can look different from classroom to classroom. Here are a few ways to include families in classroom learning:

- **Encourage families to volunteer in the classroom.** Find small tasks that parents can complete in the classroom. Use a parent volunteer form (see the Technology Resources section of this chapter for several samples) to help parents identify their strengths or areas of expertise that would contribute to the classroom community. Be sure to let families see their child engaged in rigorous activities that reinforce her skills.

- **Invite parents to participate in classroom activities.** Give families opportunities to work with their children to complete an activity. Model strategies that help the student with ASD experience success.

- **Assign home learning assignments or projects.** Home learning should reinforce objectives taught in school. These assignments should extend beyond paper-and-pencil tasks and include opportunities for parents to talk with their children about school, home, and family. To show how living things grow, students could be asked to bring in a baby photo to share. As part of the project, parents can ask the child how she has changed and what she can do now that used to be difficult. Home experiences like these build social language skills for students with ASD and help families understand learning expectations.

- **Ask families to read with their children daily.** Parents can monitor reading comprehension and fluency skills by reading with their children daily. Since many students with ASD need support in language and literacy development, this is a good way to practice these skills every day.

Working with Family Agencies

Case management agencies provide support for some students with ASD and their families. While not every family will have access to these supports, it is important to understand the role of these professionals and how they can

Checklist for Supporting Open Communication with Families of Students with ASD

Classroom families are aware of how and when they can reach me. I make myself available to speak with families before and after the school day.

     ❏ Yes   ❏ No

I produce a monthly newsletter that describes upcoming events in the classroom and school.

     ❏ Yes   ❏ No

Prior to the start of the school year, I discuss with families a preferred method of communication. I interact with families using this method as often as possible.

     ❏ Yes   ❏ No

I offer a way for families to receive regular feedback about their child's academic, social, and behavior performance in the classroom.

     ❏ Yes   ❏ No

I assist students in organizing assignments.

     ❏ Yes   ❏ No

Families are aware of home learning expectations.

     ❏ Yes   ❏ No

During the school year, I offer multiple opportunities for families to visit the classroom and participate in learning activities.

     ❏ Yes   ❏ No

I ask families for their feedback or insight before implementing new strategies or interventions.

     ❏ Yes   ❏ No

I encourage families to contact me whenever they have a concern.

     ❏ Yes   ❏ No

support the inclusion of youths with ASD. These family-based services can assist families with managing behaviors and building skills for children with developmental, emotional, or mental health needs. Family agencies typically assign each child a behavior specialist consultant (BSC) who develops a plan of care for an individual child. Each plan is implemented by a team of caseworkers.

Family agencies will sometimes work directly with schools. Both the BSC and therapeutic support staff (TSS) may visit schools to work with students with ASD. It is the job of the TSS to help the student meet goals outlined in his treatment plan. Schools provide a natural setting to work on many social and behavioral goals. In addition, these professionals can help support students in daily school activities.

Family agencies can be a tremendous resource to teachers. However, it is important to work with them professionally and appropriately. Caseworkers are not teachers and should not be expected to lead lessons. Similarly, they should not be assigned to babysit their clients while the rest of the class participates in an activity. Instead, these professionals should help students with ASD participate with the class. The BSC and TSS can also model effective ways to work with individual students. Ask questions to learn more about your student with ASD, but keep the conversation professional. Keep in mind that caseworkers are extensions of the family; speak honestly but respectfully about the student.

Establishing a Positive Relationship with Families

A positive relationship with families can go a long way toward supporting students with ASD. When a sense of trust is established between teachers and parents, families are often more committed to the efforts of the school. In addition, increased family involvement means students have greater personal resources to build skills and meet goals. Certainly, establishing positive relationships with families of children with ASD will take time, but there are many ways to initiate the process. The following are some ideas to consider:

- **Make a good first impression.** Early in the school year, invite the parents of the child with ASD for an individual meeting. Discuss your teaching philosophy, class schedules, and special routines. Be sure that families know how they can contact the school when they have concerns.

- **Celebrate success.** Inform families when students make progress. Recognize parents' influence in these gains and thank them for their support. Sharing these successes together helps to build a team atmosphere between schools and families.

- **Share the vision.** Create newsletters or organization maps that outline curricula goals for the school year. Help families understand where their child lies on the continuum of grade level expectations.

- **Use "people first" language.** No student should be identified by their disability. "People first" language puts the human being ahead of the disability—for example, it is "children from low-income backgrounds," not "poor kids." Refer to students as "children with ASD," not "autistic children" or "autistics."

- **Maintain professionalism.** As in all relationships, there will be disagreements. Many disputes can be avoided by limiting comments to factual, verifiable information (for example, "At 11:22, Sammy hit a peer," rather than "Sammy is the most aggressive child in the first grade."). Use direct observations and nonjudgmental terminology.

- **Keep promises.** Make every effort to follow through with commitments. Sticking to agreements goes a long way toward building trust with families.

- **Persist in challenges.** Teaching students with ASD can be difficult. Although frustration is understandable, the attitude you present to parents should be one of determination.

For students with ASD and typically developing students alike, families are a key component to student success. There are many ways to involve parents in the education of their children. Engaging in these practices makes classroom instruction more lasting and productive. The following strategies offer some additional ways to partner with the families of students with ASD.

Strategies to Partner with Families of Students with ASD Effectively

Teacher Brochures

Why Use This Strategy?

A child's first years of school can be a difficult transition for many families. However, parents of students with ASD often have additional stress as they help their students navigate through new school experiences. Knowing information about the teacher and her philosophy toward inclusion can help parents feel more at ease with sending their child to school.

A teacher brochure is a quick and easy way for teachers to introduce themselves to families of students with ASD. Teacher brochures can also act as a handy reference of important contact information and school event dates.

How Does This Strategy Work?

- Make a list of important information about the school, your classroom, and yourself that you want to share with families. Suggested brochure information follows.

- Organize this list into short blocks of text in a trifold brochure format.

- Distribute brochures at teacher-parent conferences or school events.

Teacher Tips

- Make sure that your teacher brochure has a professional appearance. Use a word processing template and consider adding photos or clip art. A neat, colorful appearance will make the brochure more inviting and engaging to read.

- Ask an administrative leader to review the teacher brochure before sharing it with parents. This will help ensure that the text is accurate and appropriate.

- Place school and teacher contact information prominently on the brochure. Encourage parents to reference this resource whenever they have a question or concern regarding their child's school progress.

- Review examples of teacher brochures online. Conduct an image search by typing in the words *teacher brochures for parents* in the Google toolbar.

- If feedback on the teacher brochure is positive, consider using this medium as a way to provide parents with other important information (for example, "How to Help with Homework," "How Toddlers Learn," "The Importance of Play," and so on).

Suggested Brochure Information

- *Teacher name, educational background, and teaching experience*
- *Teacher's philosophy toward teaching*
- *Special areas of teaching expertise or interests*
- *Contact information (such as email address, phone number) and preferred methods of communication*
- *Daily class schedule*
- *Special class rotation*
- *Lunch and recess times*
- *School address, phone number, fax number, school administrative assistant name*
- *School mission statement*
- *School initiatives (such as anti-bullying programing and an art-infused curricula)*
- *Special school event dates (for example, open house, holiday concerts, and parent-teacher conferences)*

Home-and-School Journals

Why Use This Strategy?

Many early childhood classrooms are busy, interactive places. Not surprisingly, very young students often struggle to keep track of daily school events. It is particularly difficult for students with ASD who may have communication needs at this age.

The home-and-school journal provides a source of regular communication between home and school. Parents and teachers can use the journal to provide each other with important information about the student with ASD. Additionally, information included in the home-and-school journal can inspire children with ASD to discuss school and home activities.

How Does This Strategy Work?

- At the end of the school day, write information about the student with ASD and her school day. Sign and date the entry.

- Ask the student's family to read your entry and select one topic from the entry to discuss with the child. For instance, if you wrote about the child's interaction with a peer at recess, the parent might ask the child to tell something about playtime.

- Have the family write a response to you about anything they wish to share about the child's evening at home. For example, they may write about how well the child slept, when she completed her homework, or how she spent free time at home.

- Read the family's entry and select one topic from the entry to discuss with the child. For example, if the parent wrote about the child's piano lesson, you might ask about what songs the student is learning to play.

Teacher Tips

- Set expectations for how often the home-and-school journal will be used at school.

It does not have to be used daily. Define a number of entries per week that is manageable and stick to it.

- Remember, the home-and-school journal is a form of documentation for teachers and parents. Always maintain a professional tone, and keep writing clear and unbiased.

- Although students' behaviors and academic progress should be a big part of the journal, you should include other important information as well. In particular, don't forget to share stories of successful social interactions with teachers and peers, gains in language or communication, and the dates and times of special school events (book fairs, school concerts, and so on).

- For very young children, consider sending the journal home with a stuffed class mascot. This may inspire interest in writing for the child if she can write about what she and the mascot did together.

- The home-and-school journal does not need to be an actual journal. Email may work better for some parents. Use electronic folders to manage and organize entries.

Strategy Sacks

Materials

Paper
Marker
Various activity materials
Bag for transporting to home

Why Use This Strategy?

Learning at home begins with parent involvement. However, many parents may not know how to best support their child's learning. The unique challenges of raising a child with ASD can make addressing learning needs at home even more complicated.

Strategy Sacks provide parents with the materials and step-by-step directions to

Sample Strategy Sack
Yellow-Line Writing (A Handwriting Strategy from Chapter 4)

Materials
Three-lined handwriting paper
Pencils
Yellow marker
Handwriting guide

Directions

- Choose a topic about which your child would like to write. Help your child think of ideas that fit with the topic you chose.

- Ask your child to say aloud the sentence she would like to write. Make sure that she says a complete sentence, not just a word or phrase.

- Using the yellow marker, write your child's response on the provided three-lined handwriting paper. Use the handwriting guide to provide proper letter formation and spacing.

- Encourage your child to trace over your handwriting.

- Ask your child to reread the sentence she wrote.

complete a grade appropriate activity. Through completion of the task, parents become more familiar with multiple ways to support or improve a particular skill.

How Does This Strategy Work?

- Select a skill that the student with ASD needs to improve.

- On paper, write step-by-step directions for completing an activity that will allow the student to practice the skill.

- Pack the materials or supplies to complete the activity in a reusable sack.

- Send the Strategy Sack home with the student.

- Have the student complete the Strategy Sack with the assistance of his family.

Teacher Tips

- Be sure to inform families when the Strategy Sack will be coming home. Set a date when the activity in the Strategy Sack should be returned to school.

- Create ownership in the activity by allowing the student to decorate or personalize the sack that holds the materials.

- Provide time in class for the student to share his completed activity with a teacher, a partner, or the class.

- Consider asking parents to provide feedback on their family's Strategy Sack experience. Ask parents to share what worked well and what was challenging.

Homework Agendas
Materials
Printouts of homework agenda template
Marker
Two-pocket folders (optional)

Why Use This Strategy?

Early childhood is an excellent time to begin building independence skills. Students with ASD, like many other young students, need practice organizing school materials and assignments. A structured classroom can help all students become more prepared for learning at home and school.

A homework agenda can be an important part of a structured early childhood classroom. Homework agendas provide students with a standard place to record homework assignments and other important school information. This type of resource can also help families support students in completing home assignments and preparing for school activities.

How Does This Strategy Work?

- Design a homework agenda that is appropriate for your grade level and classroom needs. See the sample homework agenda design that follows.

- Record daily assignments or activities in appropriate spaces on the homework agenda. Have students add special additions when appropriate.

- Ask students to take the homework agenda home with them each night. If possible, students should have a two-pocket folder to keep the homework agenda and homework assignments together in one place.

- Ask parents to monitor the homework agenda and sign it each evening.

Sample Homework Agenda Design

_____'s Homework Agenda

Date _____

Class Notes: This week, we will learn _____

_____

_____.

Monday	Tuesday	Wednesday	Thursday	Friday
How was my day? ❏ great ❏ ok ❏ needs improvement	How was my day? ❏ great ❏ ok ❏ needs improvement	How was my day? ❏ great ❏ ok ❏ needs improvement	How was my day? ❏ great ❏ ok ❏ needs improvement	How was my day? ❏ great ❏ ok ❏ needs improvement
Special Events Today: Class Assignments:	Special Events Today: Class Assignments:	Special Events Today: Class Assignments:	Special Events Today: Class Assignments:	Special Events Today: Class Assignments:
Parent Comments and Signature	Parent Comments and Signature	Parent Comments and Signature	Parent Comments and Signature	Parent Comments and Signature

- Have students return the homework agenda to school the following day.

Teacher Tips

- If you use a behavior management system in the classroom, indicate each child's daily report on the homework agenda.

- Include one or two brief sentences at the top of the homework agenda to describe weekly class learning goals. These notes can help families see meaning in home assignments.

- Be sure to include the date on the homework agenda. The design of the agenda will most likely look the same from week to week. A date will help parents recognize which homework agenda is most current.

- Let parents know that they can use homework agendas to share short notes with the teacher. Leave adequate space in each daily block for this purpose.

Letters from School
Materials
Journal notebooks

Why Use This Strategy?
Like many young children, it can be difficult for students with ASD to describe the details of their day. Delays in language along with intense focus in other interests can make discussing school events particularly challenging.

Letters from school allow families to hear about school favorites from the perspective of their child with ASD. Through a daily writing prompt, students can share what they enjoyed most about school. Not only does this strategy provide parents with a glimpse into the student's school experience, but it also offers a starting point for families to begin conversations about school.

How Does This Strategy Work?

- Discuss with the student the best part of his school day. Use several prompts to inspire conversation. Samples for letters from school prompts follow.

- In a designated journal, have the child write or dictate his response. The student can also draw a picture of his response.

- Next, ask the child to share his journal entry with a family member at home. The student and his family should discuss his response.

Teacher Tips

- Select one to two prompts to use regularly. The more frequently the child hears the prompt, the more familiar he will be with it. This will help him to understand the prompt and respond more readily.

- Try to keep journal entries as positive as possible. This is not a record of behaviors, but rather a place for the student to share things he enjoys about school.

- Add teacher details to daily entries. This will give families more information to discuss with their children. For example, if the

---

Samples for Letters from School Prompts

- *The best part of my day was _____.*
- *I really liked it when _____.*
- *I want to tell my mom/dad about _____.*
- *I did a good job today when I _____.*
- *Today I was happy when _____.*
- *Ask me about _____.*

student says that the best part of his day was lunch, the teacher might share that the child had spaghetti or talked with a new friend at his table.

- Encourage family members to provide feedback on the home discussion. Also, from time to time, ask families to help their children write about the best part of their time at home.

- Letters from home does not have to be a daily activity. Try to incorporate it into the end-of-the-day routines two to three times per week.

Photovoice
Materials
Photos from home

Why Use This Strategy?
Parents use effective strategies to help their children with ASD manage everyday activities. This insight can help teachers design adaptations for students in school. The more support and practice students with ASD have with building skills, the more likely they are to retain them.

First developed in 1992 by Caroline Wang and Mary Anne Burris to promote public health, Photovoice is now a widely used research method. Photovoice activities allow parents to share effective strategies that they use at home through a series of photographs and informal questioning.

How Does This Strategy Work?
- Ask the student's family to share a strategy that they use at home to help their child with ASD study, transition, or interact with others.

- Ask the family take photos of the strategy in use at home.

- Plan an interview or meeting with the family to review the strategy.

- Ask family members to think about the strategy directions and review the photos with other family members before attending the meeting.

- Using the photo as a guide, ask the family questions at the meeting about how the strategy works, how it is used, and how the family implements it in the home. See the sample Photovoice interview that follows.

Teacher Tips
- Be present and engaged as family members share strategies. This is an opportunity to empower the family and make them feel like contributing members of the team.

- You may also wish to use Photovoice to share a strategy used at school with families. Alternatively, Photovoice can be combined with the Strategy Sack idea on page 137.

- Follow up with the family after you use the family's strategy ideas that they shared through Photovoice. Let parents know what worked well or how you adapted the strategy.

The Meet the Family Strategy
Why Use This Strategy?
Teachers and students with ASD are not the only ones who gain from parent expertise. Peers in the classroom also want to know about their classmates with ASD. Families of students with ASD can share common experiences and likes between their children and other children in the class.

Meet the Family allows parents of students with ASD help their children share information about themselves. This information gives both the teacher and other students an opportunity to learn things about the student that might be difficult for the child to share herself. Parents can also share ways that the class can help support the student in the classroom.

How Does This Strategy Work?

- Invite a family member to speak with the class for a brief getting-to-know-you session. Keep the session under fifteen minutes, if possible.

- Ask the family member to help their child share helpful information about himself (for example, favorites, dislikes, strengths, and so on).

- Listen carefully and draw comparisons between students in the classroom. For example, if the parent mentions that the child likes action figures, the teacher might ask if other students like action figures.

Teacher Tips

- This strategy works best for students with ASD who cannot share a lot about themselves independently. It is always preferable to have the child share himself, but if that is not possible, this strategy gives the student support.

- Encourage families to bring photographs or items that might help younger students see similarities between themselves and the student with ASD.

- Respect the fact that some families may feel uncomfortable or may not want to participate in this type of activity. Offer alternative ways for families to participate.

Sample Photovoice Interview

Teacher: Can you describe for me how Colin uses this reading area?

Parent: Each colored bin represents a level of book. Books in the blue bin (number 3) are easiest. Books in the green bin (number 2) are a little harder, and books in the red bin (number 1) are the hardest. Colin can select a book based on his interest on a particular day or by level.

Teacher: Do you ever encourage Colin to select a book from the more challenging bin?

Parent: Sure.

Teacher: How do you do that?

Parent: Books from the red bin take longer for Colin to read, so we remind him that if he chooses a challenging book, he only has to read one book before he earns computer time.

Teacher: What if Colin chooses a book from the other two bins?

Parent: Colin knows that, to earn his reward, he has to read for twenty minutes each night. Do you see the numbers on each bin? Those numbers remind Colin how many books he must read from each bin. He has to read two books from the green bin, and three from the blue bin.

Teacher: Thank you for sharing this wonderful strategy with me. I can think of several ways I can use a similar system here in the classroom. I appreciate your willingness to work with me this school year!

For example, they can help the student complete an interest inventory that you can then help the student share with the class.

Technology Resources to Support Partnerships with Families

- Pinterest (https://www.pinterest.com /explore/parent-volunteer-form/) has several examples of parent volunteer forms. In addition, many free or low-cost templates are available for purchase at Teachers Pay Teachers (https://www.teacherspayteachers .com/Browse/Search:parent%20 volunteer%20forms).

- About Education (http://k6educators.about .com/od/backtoschoollessons/a/Student -Welcome-Letter.htm) provides steps for writing a welcome letter to families. The site also provides a sample welcome letter.

- Visit eHow (http://www.ehow.com /how_8288561_design-new-teacher -brochure-parents.html) for a step-by-step guide on how to create a teacher brochure. Remember, several examples of teacher brochures can be viewed by conducting a Google image search (https://images.google .com). Type "teacher brochures for parents" in the toolbar.

- Use Google Translate (https://translate .google.com/) to communicate with families who do not speak English in the home.

- As assortment of sample parent communication letters and templates are available at Real Classroom Ideas (http:// www.realclassroomideas.com/125.html).

- Suggestions for recruiting and maintaining school volunteers is available at GreatKids (http://www.greatschools.org/improvement /volunteering/577-ways-to-catch-keep -volunteers.gs?page=all). So You Want To Teach (http://www.soyouwanttoteach.com /45-tasks-for-parent-volunteers-in-the -classroom/) also has suggestions for using family volunteers in the classroom.

- Ereading Worksheets (http://www .ereadingworksheets.com/e-reading -worksheets/school-project-ideas/) suggests an alphabetical list of school project ideas that families can use to engage students in learning at home.

- A free school community tool kit is available free through Autism Speaks (http://www .autismspeaks.org/family-services/tool-kits /school-community-tool-kit). The tool kit has customized information for various members of the school community, including educators, bus drivers, custodial staff, and paraprofessionals.

- Group text services, like Remind (https:// www.remind.com/) and Kikutext (https:// kikutext.com/), allow teachers to send out information and updates to families quickly and efficiently via parents' mobile phones.

Key Terms

behavior specialist consultant (BSC): A caseworker who develops a plan of care for a student with a behavioral, emotional, or mental health disorder.

empathy: The skill of understanding and sharing in the feelings of others.

"people first" language: A way of recognizing the student first rather than the disability in written or verbal language (for example, "a student with ASD," not "an autistic student").

Photovoice: A research method that combines interviews and photographs to explain a concept, idea, or strategy.

therapeutic support staff (TSS): Caseworkers who work with a child to implement a care plan.

Professional Development for Early Childhood Educators Working with Children with ASD

Consider how the following scenario describing a preschooler's family situation might affect a new educator.

Jason works for a construction company in a rural community and, although his skills as a roofer are exemplary, his interactions with other members of the crew are problematic. In the aftermath of numerous complaints from coworkers and customers, Jason is fired from his job. At the same time, his wife of five years has filed for divorce and their three-year-old son, Preston, is beginning preschool. School personnel request a conference with the couple because they think that Preston has ASD and should be assessed by a psychologist. After learning more about the signs of autism spectrum disorders, Jason confides to a neighbor that he has ASD but it was never diagnosed. He now feels a tremendous sense of guilt about passing on "bad genes" to his son. Meanwhile, Jason's ex-wife and her family have concluded that a very expensive private school is Preston's only chance to have a "normal life." However, enrolling Preston in the program is far beyond their financial means. Ultimately, the child qualifies for and is enrolled in the local Head Start class.

Professional Development

Given Preston's family background, just imagine the huge responsibility of becoming his teacher. It extends well beyond the preschooler's academic achievement for the teacher to consider not only Preston's socioemotional functioning but also the interrelationships among his extended family members. Preston's Head Start teacher is new in every sense of the word; she is twenty years old, has just completed a two-year associate's degree, and has almost no experience with a child on the autism spectrum. Although she has a strong commitment to children and families, she experienced some issues with classroom management during her internship and is secretly fearful that Preston will be disruptive. This final chapter focuses on the steps early childhood educators can take when they don't know what to do: seek professional development.

As it applies to early childhood educators, professional development consists of all of the formal and informal learning experiences across a career that contribute to teaching effectiveness. Professional development activities for teachers are designed to enrich and enlarge professional understandings, pedagogy, disposition, and effectiveness. Figure 9.1 highlights professional development activities for teachers working with young children who have ASD and other pervasive developmental disorders.

Figure 9.1 Professional Development Activities for Teachers Working with Young Children with ASD and Other Pervasive Developmental Disorders

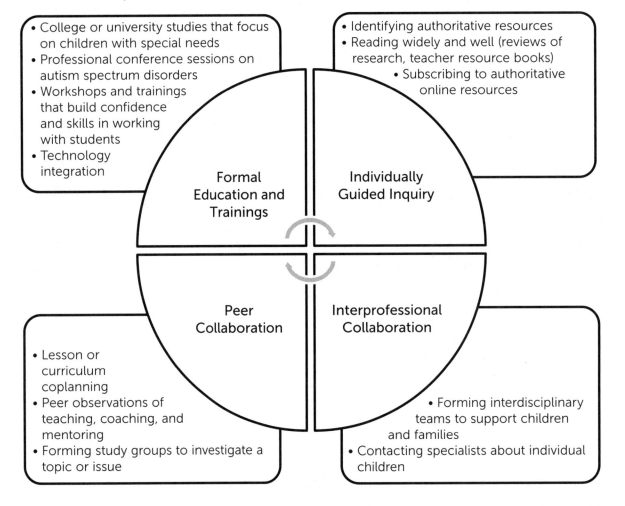

- College or university studies that focus on children with special needs
- Professional conference sessions on autism spectrum disorders
- Workshops and trainings that build confidence and skills in working with students
- Technology integration

Formal Education and Trainings

- Identifying authoritative resources
- Reading widely and well (reviews of research, teacher resource books)
- Subscribing to authoritative online resources

Individually Guided Inquiry

- Lesson or curriculum coplanning
- Peer observations of teaching, coaching, and mentoring
- Forming study groups to investigate a topic or issue

Peer Collaboration

Interprofessional Collaboration

- Forming interdisciplinary teams to support children and families
- Contacting specialists about individual children

Teacher Reflection

Most experts in the field of education regard teacher reflection as the single most important tool for professional growth. Teacher reflection refers to the ability to think about decisions and actions in the classroom and change behavior in ways that propel educators from novice to expert practice. In order to understand professional development, it is sometimes helpful to consider what would happen if it did not occur. Let's suppose that an ineffective teacher was not motivated enough to try to change her behavior. This would result in the teacher repeating that first awkward year over and over again. Three dimensions are essential to the disposition for becoming a reflective practitioner:.

- **Being wholehearted.**

  - Convey energy, enthusiasm, and dedication when teaching.

  - Expect unpredictability and challenge to be part of teaching.

  - Accept that teaching is not easy and persist at solutions.

- **Accept responsibility.**

  - Be aware of social, moral, ethical, and political issues associated with ASD.

  - Weigh consequences of own actions and admit mistakes.

  - Consider all stakeholders when making decisions.

- **Questioning assumptions.**

  - Revise thinking about ASD based on evidence.

  - Listen to others' viewpoints on PDD.

  - Respond to unexpected outcomes in ways that are helpful.

Elements of Reflective Practice in Teaching

Reflective practitioners are aware of their professional strengths and weaknesses. In 2001, the National Staff Development Council created a set of standards that all educator professional development should follow. These standards, as they apply to work with students with ASD, were developed into a checklist in table 9.1. As you read through the standards, self-assess your performance on each one. For those that are strengths, make notes on what you did to achieve a high level of performance. For those that are areas of weakness, make a plan for developing strengths and shoring up weaknesses.

General Ways to Address ASD in the Inclusive Classroom

One common concern of teachers is the rate at which a child on the autism spectrum completes a task in comparison to most other students. It is often the case that most other children will be ready to move on while the child with special needs is taking longer to finish. This creates inner conflict because the teacher feels obligated to simultaneously keep other children from losing focus and support the learning of the child with ASD. As Sian Beilock explains in her *Psychology Today* article, it is a basic psychological principle that when we are confronted with a puzzling task we frequently revert to whatever is familiar. In the classroom, students' often revert back to familiar experiences from earlier childhood and, unfortunately, teachers often resort to nagging the child or penalizing the child for these behaviors in some way. However, neither of these approaches is effective. Students can easily ignore nagging, and penalties (for example, missing playtime) can cause the child to shut down completely or, conversely, have a tantrum that disrupts the class schedule.

Table 9.1 Checklist for Rating Your Performance on National Staff Development Council Standards

Standards adapted for ASD	Rate your performance—high, medium, or low			If rated high, how did you accomplish this?	If rated medium or low, what professional development strategies can you use to improve?
Knowledge about ASD and its implications for quality teaching	H	M	L		
Selecting appropriate content and pedagogy for the student with ASD					
Making decisions based on educational research	H	M	L		
Collaboration with peers and other professionals	H	M	L		
Responsiveness to the learning needs of students with ASD in the context of an inclusive classroom	H	M	L		
Establishing and maintaining an appropriate learning environment for children with PDD	H	M	L		
Working effectively with families whose children are being evaluated or have been diagnosed	H	M	L		
Evaluation of accommodations and adaptations of teaching, curriculum, and programs to support learners with ASD	H	M	L		
Using data on individual student progress and program effectiveness to drive decision making	H	M	L		
Seeking out opportunities for learning to become a more effective teacher of the child with ASD	H	M	L		

Standards adapted from the National Staff Development Council (2001)

In order to grow professionally, early childhood educators need to change these automatic responses and replace them with actions that are effective in working with young children with ASD. Some positive, effective teacher behaviors and responses that are supported by research include the following:

● Extend wait time after questions. If you provide a bit more time, you may find that the child with ASD who did not respond immediately actually did know the answer. Rather than always insisting that an answer be in words, consider requesting that an answer be a behavior (for example, "Stand up if you like pizza."). Allowing this way of responding can encourage participation.

● Provide visual reminders to help children focus and follow instructions. Don't overwhelm children with ASD with words; keep speech clear and direct (for example, by saying "Marquis—your mittens" and touching the mittens as a way to remind him to put on mittens before going outside to play).

● Demonstrate how a task is completed rather than relying on words alone. For example, instead of simply telling children to fold a piece of paper lengthwise, say, "First, let's fold our paper in the longer, skinnier way—like a hot dog bun," and actually show the class how to do this.

- Use real objects or representations of objects while giving explanations. For example, rather than telling children how to use the headphones at the listening center, ask for volunteers from the class to perform each action while operating the equipment.

- Model how to initiate responses with peers. For example, have the children use stuffed toys to show how to come up and merge with ongoing play instead of disrupting it. It is sometimes better to coach children with ASD to merge with the ongoing play than to tell them to explicitly ask if they can play. Try role-playing to practice merging with ongoing play. For instance, if other children are playing with blocks, the child who wants to join in takes blocks from the shelf, sits down, and begins playing with blocks alongside the others. But—and this is the important part—she does not knock down the other children's structures or take away the blocks they have arranged in front of them. You can coach children to do this by suggesting that they "stop, look, and copycat."

- Use the child's intense interests as a way to focus attention. For example, if the lesson is about dinosaurs and a child with ASD is fascinated by them, use this as an opportunity to enlist cooperation. You might announce that you will introduce each of the dinosaurs first and, if everyone pays attention, they will be placed on the carpet during playtime.

- Check for understanding more often. Begin the lesson with a list of what will occur (in pictures and in print) and, rather than waiting until the lesson is completely over to ask "Are there any questions?" pause periodically and ask someone to recap what they learned so far while you point out those things on the list.

- Ask children to respond using more than one modality (for example, with a puppet, in a role play, via a drawing, and so on). Special education has a long history of encouraging multiple ways of responding to support inclusion. Children with ASD should be allowed different ways of showing what they know. If a particular child does not use spoken language much, computer software might be a way they can respond or a way to rehearse for the real thing. For example, the Toca Tea Party app (https://tocaboca.com/apps/) allows children to create a virtual tea party before participating in a real one. Likewise, an app called Sock Puppets (http://my.smithmicro.com/sock-puppets-description.html) allows students to create a puppet show on screen before making a sock puppet and using it.

Strategies to Promote Professional Development in Educators of Young Students with ASD

Skills of Colleagueship

What Are Skills of Colleagueship?
Part of professional development is becoming a valued colleague who establishes positive relationships with fellow teachers, administrators, and professionals from other fields. Given the complexity of ASD, outcomes for children and families are affected by colleagueship and collaboration.

Colleagues take responsibility for their own actions, yet have a commitment to others as well as to the goals of the program. Helpful strategies for working with colleagues to support students with ASD are noted by Donald

Graves in his article in *Language Arts,* and by Mary Renck Jalongo and Joan Isenberg in their book *Creative Thinking and Arts-Based Learning.*

The strategies these educators suggest include the following:

- Putting children's and families' needs first
- Being committed to equity and fairness
- Being trustworthy with confidential and important information
- Considering other points of view thoughtfully
- Volunteering and stepping up
- Having energy and enthusiasm
- Having a sense of humor
- Avoiding laying the blame on others
- Celebrating successes
- Recognizing failure and striving for continuous improvement
- Noticing what others do well
- Knowing when and who to ask for advice and support
- Being avid learners
- Being dependable and trustworthy
- Knowing others as people, not just as coworkers
- Sharing books, ideas, and other resources
- Talking about interests beyond teaching
- Having a vision of where they are headed personally and professionally
- Being candid, yet diplomatic
- Supporting ideas with evidence rather than defensiveness
- Knowing when to take a stand and when to go along
- Having the ability to disagree without rancor

- Offering good problem-solving strategies
- Acknowledging mistakes and genuinely striving to do better

How Does This Strategy Work?

- Build reciprocal trust and respect. As you work with others, try to avoid judging or blaming. For example, teachers sometimes complain that a professional from another field just doesn't understand their daily responsibilities and experiences with a child. This is probably true; a psychologist or speech-language pathologist will look at things differently, but this is a strength of interprofessional collaboration because "none of us is as smart as all of us." It is not necessary for everyone to look at the case of a child with ASD in exactly the same way in order to support the child and family. Disagreement and differing viewpoints don't mean the relationship has to be adversarial, however. Accept that there will be times when you will not achieve consensus and "agree to disagree."

- Recognize that being a good colleague is more than being nice. Actually, a responsible colleague accepts that some conversations with other professionals will be difficult. For example, if a coworker is habitually late, it might be easier to shrug it off (or complain to someone else) but a responsible colleague will be candid and speak directly to that person. Assume that anything you say will somehow get back to that person because, usually, it does. Most people are justifiably upset when they learn of others talking "behind their backs" or "going over their heads." Although it is more stressful to talk to the person directly, that is what responsible colleagues do.

- Try to spare others further embarrassment. Just as you would tell a person if they had spinach stuck to their front teeth, you should gently warn a colleague if you see them about to make a mistake. For example, a preschool teacher was working with a student teacher who wanted to use the rhythm band instruments as part of her lesson. However, this novice made the procedural error of distributing the instruments first and expecting the children not to experiment with them while she gave them instructions. As a result, she kept stopping to remind the children not to touch the instruments. Afterwards, the experienced teacher gently inquired, "If you were teaching this lesson again tomorrow, what would you do differently?" and the student teacher was well aware of what went wrong.

Active Listening

Why Use This Strategy?

Active listening refers to a set of habits that demonstrate a sincere effort to hear, understand, and respond in appropriate ways when communicating with others. Some of the behaviors associated with active listening include keeping quiet and still, staying alert, and making eye contact. Active listening at a professional gathering also includes taking notes, listening to understand, posing thoughtful questions, asking for clarification when necessary, and paraphrasing and recapping as a check of understanding.

How Does This Strategy Work?

- Conduct this listening self-assessment. Invite a colleague to talk about a topic that she is very interested in for two minutes. Time yourself and see if you can truly listen without interrupting, getting distracted by your own thinking, or mentally rehearsing what you will say when the speaker is finished. This task frequently is much harder than people imagine.

- Make an effort to display the behaviors associated with careful listening during meetings. These include such things as sitting up straight and keeping still, looking at the speaker, leaning forward slightly, taking notes, turning off electronic devices, and refusing to engage in side conversations.

- Practice ways of talking that reflect careful listening. Pose thoughtful questions rather than talking too much. Some indicators of careful listening are not repeating a question that was already answered, requesting information/clarification when confusion occurs, and asking questions that bring the group back if it seems to be drifting from its purpose.

- Disagree respectfully. Diplomacy is important when your thinking is at odds with what you are hearing. For example, if a parent suggests corporal punishment for the child as a solution, this is something you cannot support. However, you do not want to alienate the parent by vehemently disagreeing. You might say something such as, "Parents sometimes think that they need to lay down the law and this will solve the problem, but after working with young children on the autism spectrum for many years and studying the research, I've learned that . . ." or, suggest an alternative: "Many young children with autism will shut down completely when those they trust grow frustrated or angry. You may question this approach, but I wonder if . . . ."

- Avoid misunderstandings. At various points in the meeting, check for comprehension. Methods for checking for comprehension include restating what has been said, summarizing the conclusions reached, and clarifying each person's responsibilities in working toward a solution. This is especially important for IEP meetings.

Listening and Reading Comprehension Research-Based Methods

Why Use This Strategy?

One of the major trends in education today is making decisions based on research and evidence rather than instinct, tradition, or convenience. Educators throughout the world are attending conference sessions on evidence-based methods of teaching and data-driven decision-making. For example, student teachers in early childhood education were planning lessons for students enrolled in area preschools. One idea was to read John Scieszka's book *The True Story of the Three Little Pigs by A. Wolf.* When asked why they had selected their activities, the student teachers indicated that they did these activities when they were in school and liked them. Their professor pointed out that for children to understand this version of "The Three Little Pigs," they would first need to know the original story. The professor asked: Based on what you know about young children's development, do you expect them to understand satire?

In this example, the preservice educators relied on what is familiar rather than what is supported in the research. Language delays and disorders frequently are observed in young children with ASD. Efforts to support the child's growth in language are further complicated by the fact that language is not only an academic skill, but also a tool for social interaction. Research on listening and reading comprehension suggests that, in order to understand a message, children need to practice the following skills:

- Maintaining a focus while reading
- Linking prior knowledge with the reading selection
- Understanding characters' motives and intentions

- Understanding abstract words (for example, *kind* and *brave*)
- Making predictions or inferences
- Identifying cause-effect relationships
- Getting the gist of the story

How Does This Strategy Work?

Research-based strategies that early childhood educators can use to support listening and reading comprehension include the following:

- Build on the child's experience. Use warm-up activities first to activate prior knowledge, such as using cue cards to depict a scene and cards for the basic emotions in the scene; have the child choose the correct card (for example, "Jimmy loved to ride his tricycle on the sidewalk but now it is broken. Who had a broken tricycle? Will Jimmy be able to ride it? Which card shows how Jimmy feels—happy, sad, or afraid?"). Relate the text to what they know from everyday experiences (for example, "You saw dinosaur bones on our field trip, right?" "Who else do you know who likes to play outside?"). Pose questions such as, "Tell me everything you know about . . . ." Model the use of starter phrases such as, "I see . . . ," "Here is . . . ," and "I like . . . ."

- Choose simple, concrete ideas. Try using books with simple, clear pictures and stories in which the good/bad characters are obvious rather than subtle. Use animated texts to point out observable behaviors that reflect motives and intentions—for example, a chicken flapping its wings to show agitation.

- Focus attention. Set a clear purpose before the text is shared. Choose books that are more interactive (for example, flaps to lift, slots to pull, or textures to feel). Capitalize on the child's interests when making reading selections to build motivation. Use a variety of graphic organizers to focus attention on what is important for understanding (for example, a chart of *Who, What, When, Where,* and *Why*).

- Provide repetition and multisensory approaches. Use cumulative tales (for example, "The House That Jack Built") to help the child get the point of the book and to review the sequence of events.

- Try making a storyboard of the story. Dramatize an important scene from the book. Use clip-art images to make the meaning of the story more evident. Engage the child in retelling the story afterwards by referring back to the pictures.

- Model thinking aloud. Demonstrate how readers make inferences, using words such as "It looks like they are going to . . . ," "I predict that . . . ," "I wonder what will happen after . . . ," "If ____, then ____." Use predictable books to build the child's confidence in making predictions. Have the child read with a partner who does this well. Reread a book to give the child practice with identifying clues to the outcome of the story. Invite children to use drawings or diagrams to make cause/effect relationships more concrete.

- Recap to strengthen understanding. After reading, present the child with pictures of characters and have the student suggest thoughts or words from that character to fill in cartoon-type speech or thought bubbles (these are available in Microsoft Word as callouts).

Inquiry-Based Learning about ASD
Materials
Various materials depending on activity

Why Use This Strategy?
Inquiry-based learning refers to self-directed study intended to answer important questions.

The sources of that learning may be print, non-print, or human. High-quality resources about ASD can benefit early childhood educators in the following ways:

- Explain ASD in accurate, simple terms that others—both adults and children—can understand.

- Provide support to teachers in inclusive settings by offering sound advice on behavior management, lesson planning, and assessment.

- Convey a message of respect for differences and a shared responsibility for helping children on the autism spectrum to achieve their full potential.

- Help teachers to understand and empathize with the challenges that children with ASD and their families face.

How Does This Strategy Work?

- Review key resources and recommend them to families. When parents first learn of their child's diagnosis, they may be worried about their child's future, fearful that their child will be rejected by peers, angry with the professionals who delivered the message, or unsure about what they can do. Part of developing professionally is providing the right support at the right time for parents. It will do little good to thrust reading materials into their hands when they are overwhelmed, but later on providing print and online resources can be exactly what they need. For example, the book *An Early Start for Your Child with Autism: Using Everyday Activities to Help Kids Connect, Communicate, and Learn* was written by intervention specialists Sally Rogers, Geraldine Dawson, and Laurie Vismara, who work specifically with toddlers and preschoolers with ASD and their families.

- Discover the best picture books for children with various developmental disorders. High-quality picture books that have earned the recognition of highly-regarded professional groups explain ASD and other pervasive developmental disorders in simple terms. Teachers can rely on them to provide developmentally appropriate information, model acceptance of differences, and demonstrate coping strategies. Look for picture books that have earned awards from special education groups, such as the Dolly Gray Award given by the Council for Exceptional Children (http://daddcec.org/Awards/DollyGrayAwards.aspx). Likewise, National Autism Resources (www.nationalautismresources.com/autism-childrens-books.html) provides a list of the best picture books for children, and the Autism Speaks website recommends books written in Spanish (https://www.autismspeaks.org/family-services/resource-library/books).

- Read to develop professionally. Several groups identify the most helpful resources for teachers, including Autism Support Network, Friendship Circle, and those listed on the websites of leading professional organizations. Watch for books that earn positive reviews and add them to your reading list, such as *Ten Things Every Child with Autism Wishes You Knew*.

- Try Universal Design for Learning (UDL) to support accommodations and adaptations. UDL is a way to meet individual needs within a diverse group of students. Foundational to the principles of UDL is the concept of maximizing access to learning and the curriculum for all students, not just those identified as having disabilities. UDL responds to differences through flexibility

in how children will engage in an activity, demonstrate their understanding, and get feedback on their work. In a lesson developed by a Head Start teacher, for example, the objective was for children to understand the sequence and setting in a simple story. She selected the book *Cheer Up, Mouse* by Jed Henry, in which a series of animal friends try to get their friend out of the doldrums by performing various physical actions. The teacher identified several different ways for children to participate and demonstrate understanding:

- Watch the book trailer (just type "Cheer Up, Mouse! by Jed Henry" into the toolbar of YouTube). Then, talk about why the animals' ideas of fun are unique.

- Use small replicas of the animals (bird, frog, badger, hedgehog, rabbit, and mole) to enact the story.

- Make cue cards of the animals' actions (for example, flap and flutter, dip and dive, splash and paddle, wash and wade) so that children can perform the actions as the story is read.

- Play a matching game that pairs each animal to its habitat. Make it self-correcting by putting matching stickers on the back and laminating the cards. (Type "Cheer Up, Mouse images" into a browser to find pictures to download.)

- Schedule individual appointments for each child to work with a volunteer and aide to retell the story verbally using a set of picture cards or to draw or dictate the story. In this way, every child can participate in learning the story as well as demonstrate his understanding of the story.

Interprofessional Collaboration

Why Use This Strategy?

Interprofessional collaboration refers to direct interaction between at least two equal parties voluntarily participating in shared decision-making as they work toward a common objective. Some common situations during which this would occur include meetings that involve more than one of the following types of professionals: teachers—general education teachers and teachers with specific training, such as special education teachers, music, art, or physical education teachers; school administrators; and professionals in addition to school personnel, such as occupational therapists, speech/language pathologists, psychologists, counselors, and social workers.

Interprofessional collaboration contributes to a teacher's professional growth because each person on the team brings something different in terms of training, perspective, experience, and strength. Interactions among professionals help teachers who are less experienced acquire on-the-job-training skills necessary to support the child with a pervasive developmental disorder along with her family. Research on interprofessional collaboration by Amy Kelly and Matt Tincani indicates that this approach can lead to improved outcomes for clients and children. For example, when child care providers contribute their daily observations of children's behavior to the discussion, it enables the entire team to propose accommodations and adaptations that are more beneficial to the child. Likewise, when teachers who have extensive experience assist those who do not, both can benefit. Novices get the support that they need from coaches while the coaches are recognized for their expertise.

How Does This Strategy Work?

There are several key elements of interprofessional collaboration that teachers can use to make the most of meetings.

- Establish a shared purpose. When a group convenes, begin by stating the meeting's purpose and goals. Positive professional relationships that support children with autism are achieved when there is consensus that the purpose of the meeting is to enhance opportunities for the child rather than to blame or criticize. Take the time to prepare a meeting agenda. An agenda can make the meeting more efficient, keep the focus on student and family needs, emphasize the meeting's specific purpose, generate a list of tasks, and assign roles to the participants so that everyone shoulders responsibility. A meeting agenda overview, adapted from Jacqueline Thousand and Richard Villa's book *Collaborative Teams* and an article in *Early Childhood Education Journal* by Juliet Hart Barnett and Kaitlin O'shaughnessy, follows.

- Build reciprocal trust and respect. Too often, people in a group try to find allies and respond to those they regard as most similar to them in outlook. However, when the goal is to support inclusion for a child with a disability, a chorus of professional opinion is more beneficial than a single point of view. Just as inclusion is promoted in the classroom, inclusion needs to be reflected during interprofessional interactions. If a person from one field seems to lack knowledge about the role of a person from a different field, it is an opportunity to educate one another rather than allow a communication breakdown to derail the process.

- Use multiple methods of contact. Each member of the team has a different schedule and priorities. When the group uses varied ways of connecting, such as informal hallway conversations, email messages, telephone contacts, and meeting reminders, this helps to reduce the problem of someone failing to receive an important message.

Figure 9.2 Coplanning Meeting Agenda Template

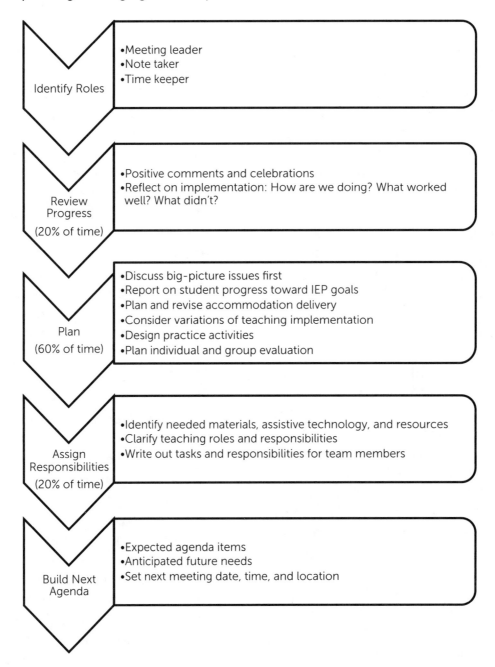

Identify Roles
- Meeting leader
- Note taker
- Time keeper

Review Progress
(20% of time)
- Positive comments and celebrations
- Reflect on implementation: How are we doing? What worked well? What didn't?

Plan
(60% of time)
- Discuss big-picture issues first
- Report on student progress toward IEP goals
- Plan and revise accommodation delivery
- Consider variations of teaching implementation
- Design practice activities
- Plan individual and group evaluation

Assign Responsibilities
(20% of time)
- Identify needed materials, assistive technology, and resources
- Clarify teaching roles and responsibilities
- Write out tasks and responsibilities for team members

Build Next Agenda
- Expected agenda items
- Anticipated future needs
- Set next meeting date, time, and location

- Manage conflict appropriately. Another important relationship-building tool is learning to disagree without rancor. Sometimes, people have fallen into the destructive habit of agreeing in public so that they are seen as someone who is easy to work with and then hold a meeting after the meeting to air their real feelings and bitter complaints. One proactive way of dealing with unnecessary conflict is to periodically paraphrase and double-check meaning rather than assume that everyone has heard and understood.

- Share accountability. Part of working collaboratively is to be genuinely interested in one another's skills, experiences, interests, and educational philosophies—all with an eye toward equality in the relationship. When collaborative groups form, it is very important to distribute the work among the members of the group so that everyone becomes a stakeholder in the outcomes for the child and family. For more ideas, visit the website of the Center for Effective Collaboration and Practice (http://cecp.air.org/schools_special.asp).

Responding to Families' Questions and Identifying Community Resources
Why Use This Strategy?
In a majority of instances, parents of children with ASD first notice their child's difficulties by eighteen months of age and seek help by the time the child is two years old. Behaviors sometimes noted by parents of children with ASD include such things as language delays, communication difficulties, disinterest in social

Example of Identifying Community Resources: Assistance Dogs

Teachers often find that families ask them for their opinions about the value of various interventions that might help a child with ASD. One intervention that has received considerable attention in the media recently is companion dogs for children with pervasive developmental delays and disorders. Not all children with ASD are good candidates for an assistance dog. The partnership between the child and dog has to be reciprocal, and the adults in the family have to make a commitment to the care and training of the animal as well. In order for the dog-child pair to be effective, the child has to be capable of treating the dog kindly and the dog has to want to stay close to the child. For higher-functioning children with pervasive developmental disorders or delays, the child would participate in training together with the animal and learn to use simple commands. When a child and assistance dog form a reciprocal bond, it sometimes leads to breakthroughs in the child's ability to express affection or attempt to communicate in words. Because the dog is a living thing, the common ground of affection for the animal can build a bridge of understanding between the child with ASD and other family members. For some children who are not as high functioning, dogs can be trained to assist adults; for example, to alert them if the child wanders off.

Educators can support families by locating information and researching community resources.

- **Lead the family to authoritative resources.** Assistance dogs for children with ASD require a considerable investment of time, effort, travel, and money. There are, however, groups that will provide financial support. Families need to understand that the dogs are raised as puppies, trained for a year or more, and then trained to support the specific child. Encourage families to consult the websites of respected professional organizations, such as:

  - Service Dogs at Autism Speaks
    https://www.autismspeaks.org/services/service-dogs?page=2
    Contains numerous articles and videos about children with ASD and their assistance dogs.

    (continued)

- Indiana Canine Assistant Dogs (ICAN)
  http://www.icandog.org/autism-assistance-dogs
  Describes the ways in which assistance dogs for children with ASD are trained and provides information about the potential benefits of canine companions for the child and the family.

- Assistance Dogs for Autism
  http://autismassistancedog.com/service-dog-training/service-dog-application-process-2/
  Explains the process of acquiring an autism assistance dog in considerable detail.

- United Disabilities Services Foundation
  http://www.udservices.org/services/support-programs-and-services/service-dogs/
  Describes service dog training and the benefits for clients.

- Advise families to talk with other, well-informed and experienced families who have successfully integrated an autism assistance dog into their families.

- Explore reputable service dog training in your community. Be aware that there are many unscrupulous groups that claim to provide service dogs but are just money-making schemes that lead to disappointment. Reputable organizations typically:
  - Provide dogs that are thoroughly health-checked and temperament-tested
  - Have earned the endorsements of leading professional associations and have a record of producing many successful child-dog teams
  - Require at least one year of training for the dog and a period of personalized/supervised training in which the child, a parent, and the dog all participate
  - Match clients with dogs very carefully and thoughtfully
  - Replace or remove the dog if necessary and balance their commitment to the child with an obligation to do right by the animal

- Advocate for the child, family, and animal. If a child with ASD already has an assistance dog or acquires one, encourage the family to bring the dog to visit the school if possible. If allergies are a concern, it might be possible to have the dog professionally groomed prior to the presentation (this reduces animal dander) and to go outdoors for the visit (in this way, allergens are dispersed through the air instead of in a confined space). Even if the dog is not permitted to accompany the child to school, the student can share about their assistance dog with the other children through a film or still photographs. You might suggest that the family create a movie with a voice-over that describes the child with ASD and her relationship with the assistance dog. Or suggest that the child and family make a slide show to share on the computer, or a picture book using photographs of the dog to place in the reading area. Advise the family to emphasize the things that the dog can do for the child and the activities that they enjoy together, because this will encourage other students to identify with the student with ASD. Realize that dogs who are bonded to children with ASD can help the child's peers see her in a different way—not as deficient, but as truly special. Dogs are also widely known to function as a "social lubricant"—in other words, people without disabilities are more inclined to smile and talk to a person with a disability when a dog is present.

interaction, hypersensitivity to sensory stimuli (for example, clothing, noises, changes in routines), repetitive behaviors (for example, flapping hands, rocking, nonsense words). When families go in search of help, the responses of the professionals—particularly the child's teachers—need to focus not only on supplying the most authoritative and up-to-date information, but also on responding appropriately to family members' needs for reassurance and understanding.

How Does This Strategy Work?
Before you can genuinely support children and families, you need to do several things.

- Try to identify with the family. It is important to imagine yourself in their situation rather than judge them. A child is not a label, a diagnosis, or a problem and should never be treated as such. Do some reading of the candid and heartfelt accounts written by families and adults on the autism spectrum who once were children in schools. Autism Resources (http://www.autism-resources .com/) includes factual materials but also a wide variety of books and movies that families may find helpful. Suggest that parents who have recently learned their child has ASD read other parents' answers to the question, "I just discovered my child is autistic. What should I do?" in the Advice to Parents memo.

- Locate family-friendly resources. Parents and families have many questions about how their child was diagnosed, what the diagnosis means, which types of interventions are recommended, and so on. Online resources that are specifically tailored for parents include the following:

  - Autism Web (http://www.autismweb .com/) explains various disorders, educational methods, special diets, and resources.

  - Talk about Curing Autism (http:// www.tacanow.org/) supports families of newly diagnosed children with information and resources.

  - OASIS: Online Asperger Syndrome Information and Support (http://www .aspergersyndrome.org/) links to local, national, and international help and services as well as news, forums, articles, and a bookstore.

  - Autism Resources by State (http://www .autism-pdd.net/autism-resources-by -state/) helps families locate supports in their geographic region.

- Be hopeful as well as helpful. It is not enough to give families facts and figures about autism. They also need to know how teachers can help, how they can help, and that there are reasons for hope. It is important to make families aware of the many admired and successful individuals who have had ASD.

Technology Resources to Support Professional Development for Educators of Young Students with ASD

- Autism National Committee (http://www .autcom.org) offers public policy and research information.

- Autism-PDD Resource Network (http://www .autism-pdd.net/) is designed to raise public awareness of issues pertaining to autism spectrum disorders. It provides insight and supports efforts to learn more about autism.

- Autism Resources Frequently Asked Questions (http://www.autism-resources .com/autism.faq.html) includes definitions and descriptions of autism and Asperger syndrome, a glossary of terms and acronyms, lists of related disorders, treatments, books, movies, history, organizations, initiatives, and so on. Advice to parents who discover their child is autistic is provided from other parents.

- The Easter Seals (http://www.easterseals.com /explore-resources/living-with-autism/) What Is Autism? section answers many questions, such as who is most likely to be on the spectrum, and defines terminology, such as Rett syndrome and PDD.

- The IRIS Center (http://iris.peabody .vanderbilt.edu/) is a group whose mission is improving education outcomes for all children (from birth through age twenty-one), especially those with disabilities, through the use of effective evidence-based practices and interventions.

- Some sites that report on autism research are Interactive Autism Network (http://www .iancommunity.org/cs/about_asds/pddnos), Research Autism (http://www.researchautism .net/), and Organization for Autism Research (OAR) (http://www.researchautism.org).

- Families for Early Autism Treatment (FEAT) (http://www.feat.org/) is a nonprofit agency that consists of parents, professionals, and family members of those on the autism spectrum. You can find information for several states on this site. Each state-specific page discusses the upcoming events for

that area. There is a document library which offers information on treatment, practices, and laws regarding those with autism.

- Help with Autism, Asperger's Syndrome & Related Disorders (http://www.autism-help .org/index.htm) is a very practical website from Australia. It provides free general information on autism and Asperger syndrome to families, health professionals, and to the community. Included on the site are fact sheets, ways to deal with behavioral issues, personal stories, and links to family support resources.

- The Center on Response to Intervention (http://www.rti4success.org/) has a wide array of teaching strategies and helpful videos posted to their website.

- The National Institute of Neurological Disorders and Stroke (http://www.ninds.nih .gov/disorders/autism/detail_autism.htm) provides an autism spectrum disorder fact sheet. This fact sheet provides a synopsis of what is currently understood about ASD (NIH Publication No. 09–1877).

- Talk about Curing Autism (http://www .tacanow.org/) is for families of children who have been newly diagnosed. It includes links for family resources, the newly diagnosed, and autism facts.

Key Terms

active listening: Listening that goes beyond hearing a message to achieve full understanding of the speaker's point of view as well as "reading between the lines" to glimpse the tone of the message.

colleagueship: Positive, professional relationships among people who work together, either because they have the same employer or because they share a responsibility.

interprofessional collaboration: Teamwork of a diverse group of professionals built on reciprocal trust and respect that is focused on achieving important outcomes for children and families.

professional development: The process of becoming a more, rather than less, effective teacher with additional experience and time in the role. Professional development for teachers signifies growth in key areas such as knowledge, pedagogy (teaching children), and commitment to children, families, and the profession.

reflective practice: The ability to thoughtfully consider professional behaviors and revise them as necessary to achieve better outcomes for students.

References and Resources

American Occupational Therapy Association. 2010. "The Scope of Occupational Therapy Services for Individuals with an Autism Spectrum Disorder Across the Life Course." *American Journal of Occupational Therapy* 64: S125–36.

American Psychiatric Association. 2013. *Diagnostic and Statistical Manual of Mental Disorders*. 5th ed., Rev. ed. Arlington, VA: American Psychiatric Association Publishing.

Attwood, Tony. 2003. "Understanding and Managing Circumscribed Interests." In *Learning and Behavior Problems in Asperger Syndrome*, edited by Margot Prior, 126–47. New York: The Guilford Press.

Baker, Jed, ed. 2008. *No More Meltdowns: Positive Strategies for Managing and Preventing Out-of-Control Behavior.* Arlington, TX: Future Horizons.

Banda, Devender R., Eric Grimmett, and Stephanie L. Hart. 2009. "Activity Schedules." *Teaching Exceptional Children* 41(4): 16–21.

Barnett, Juliet E. Hart, and Kaitlin O'shaughnessy. 2015. "Enhancing Collaboration Between Occupational Therapists and Early Childhood Educators Working with Children on the Autism Spectrum." *Early Childhood Education Journal* 43(6): 467–72.

Beilock, Sian. 2011. "Flocking to the Familiar Under Stress." *Psychology Today,* June 15, https://www .psychologytoday.com/blog/choke/201106/ flocking-the-familiar-under-stress

Blackwell, Ann J., and T. F. McLaughlin. 2005. "Using Guided Notes, Choral Responding, and Response Cards to Increase Student Performance." *International Journal of Special Education* 20(2): 1–5.

Boshoff, Kobie, and Hugh Stewart. 2013. "Key Principles for Confronting the Challenges of Collaboration." *Exceptional Children* 70: 167–84.

Boucher, Cheryl, and Kathy Oehler. 2013. *"I Hate to Write!": Tips for Helping Students with Autism Spectrum and Related Disorders Increase Achievement, Meet Academic Standards, and Become Happy, Successful Writers.* Lenexa, KS: AAPC.

Branson, Diane, Debra C. Vigil, and Ann Bingham. 2008. "Community Childcare Providers' Role in the Early Detection of Autism Spectrum Disorders." *Early Childhood Education Journal* 35(6): 523–30.

Carnahan, Christina R., Pamela S. Williamson, and Jennifer Christman. 2011. "Linking the Cognition and Literacy in Students with Autism Spectrum Disorder." *Teaching Exceptional Children* 43(6): 54–62.

Centers for Disease Control and Prevention. 2015. "Data & Statistics," accessed August 31, 2015. http://www .cdc.gov/ncbddd/autism/data.html

Centers for Disease Control and Prevention. 2015. "Facts About ASD," accessed August 31, 2015. http://www .cdc.gov/ncbddd/autism/facts.html

Cohen, Shirley. 2006. *Targeting Autism: What We Know, Don't Know, and Can Do to Help Young Children with Autism Spectrum Disorder.* 3rd ed. Berkeley, CA: University of California Press.

Conderman, Greg, Sarah Johnston-Rodriguez, and Paula Hartman. 2009. "Communicating and Collaborating in Co-Taught Classrooms." *Teaching Exceptional Children Plus* 5(5). http://files.eric.ed.gov/fulltext/EJ967751.pdf

Denkyirah, Anthony M., and Wilson K. Agbeke. 2010. "Strategies for Transitioning Preschoolers with Autism Spectrum Disorders to Kindergarten." *Early Childhood Education Journal* 38(4): 265–70.

DiCarlo, Cynthia F., and Kamille J. Watson. 2015. "Increasing Completion of Classroom Routines Through the Use of Picture Activity Schedules." *Early Childhood Education Journal* 44(2): 88–96.

Edelson, Stephen M. 2015. "Learning Styles and Autism." *Autism Research Institute,* accessed August 31, 2015. www.autism.com/index.php/understanding_learning

Feldman, Jean. 2000. *Transition Tips and Tricks for Teachers: Attention-Grabbing Creative Activities that are Sure to Become Classroom Favorites.* Lewisville, NC: Gryphon House.

Friend, Marilyn Penovich, and Lynne Cook. 2013. *Interactions: Collaboration Skills for School Professionals.* 7th ed. Boston, MA: Pearson.

Gal, Eynat, Murray Dyck, and Anne Passmore. 2002. "Sensory Differences and Stereotyped Movements in Children with Autism." *Behaviour Change* 19(4): 207–19.

Gamliel, Ifat, and Nurit Yirmiya. 2008. "Assessment of Social Behavior in Autism Spectrum Disorders." In *Assessment of Autism Spectrum Disorders,* edited by Sam Goldstein, Jack A. Naglieri, and Sally Ozonoff, 138–70. New York: The Guilford Press.

Gargiulo, Richard M. 2015. *Special Education in Contemporary Society.* Thousand Oaks, CA: Sage.

Grandin, Temple. 2006. *Thinking in Pictures: My Life with Autism.* 2nd ed. New York: Vintage Books.

Graves, Donald H. 2001. "Build Energy with Colleagues." *Language Arts* 79(1): 12–19.

Gray, Carol. 1994. *Comic Strip Conversations.* Arlington, TX: Future Horizons.

Gray, Carol. 2001. *My Social Stories Book.* London, UK: Jessica Kingsley.

Hampshire, Patricia. K., and Jack J. Hourcade. 2012. "Teaching Play Skills to Children with Autism Using Visually Structured Tasks." *Teaching Exceptional Children* 46(3): 26–31.

Harste, Jerome C., Kathy Gnagey Short, and Carolyn L. Burke. 1988. *Creating Classrooms for Authors.* Portmouth, NH: Heinemann.

Hart, Juliet E. 2013. "Misbehavior or Missed Opportunity? Challenges in Interpreting the Behavior of Young Children with Autism Spectrum Disorder." *Early Childhood Education Journal* 41(4): 257–63.

Henry, Jed. 2014. *Cheer Up, Mouse.* Boston, MA: HMH Books.

Individuals with Disabilities Education Improvement Act (IDEA) of 2004. Public Law 108–446, 20 U.S.C.

Jackson, Phillip W. 1968. *Life in the Classroom.* New York: Holt, Reinhart, & Winston.

Jalongo, Mary Renck. 2013. *Early Childhood Language Arts.* 6th ed. Boston, MA: Allyn & Bacon.

Jensen, Eric. 2005. *Teaching with the Brain in Mind.* 2nd ed., Rev. ed. Alexandria, VA: ASCD.

Kelly, Amy, and Matt Tincani. 2013. "Collaborative Training and Practice Among Applied Behavior Analysts Who Support Individuals with Autism Spectrum Disorder." *Education and Training in Autism and Developmental Disabilities* 48:120–131.

Klipper, Barbara. 2014. *Programming for Children and Teens with Autism Spectrum Disorder.* Chicago, IL: ALA.

Kluth, Paula. 2013. *Don't We Already Do Inclusion?: One Hundred Ideas for Improving Inclusive Schools.* Cambridge, WI: Cambridge Book Review.

Kluth, Paula, and Patrick Schwarz. 2008. *Just Give Him the Whale.* Baltimore, MD: Brookes.

Koegel, Lynn Kern, Robert L. Koegel, William Frea, and Israel Green-Hopkins. 2003. "Priming as a Method of Coordinating Educational Services for Students with Autism." *Language, Speech, and Hearing Services in Schools* 34(3): 228–35.

Kutscher, Martin L. 2014. *Kids in the Syndrome Mix of ADHD, LD, Autism Spectrum, Tourette's, Anxiety, and More: The One-Stop Guide for Parents, Teachers, and Other Professionals.* London, UK: Jessica Kingsley.

Luyster, Rhiannon J., Mary Beth Kadlec, Alice Carter, and Helen Tager-Flusberg. 2008. "Language Assessment and Development in Toddlers with Autism Spectrum Disorders." *Journal of Autism and Developmental Disorders* 38(8): 1426–38.

Matson, Johnny L., and Marie Nebel-Schwalm. 2007. "Assessing Challenging Behaviors in Children with Autism Spectrum Disorders: A Review." *Research in Developmental Disabilities* 28(6): 567–79.

McIntyre, Laura Lee. 2011. "Kindergarten Transition Preparation: A Comparison of Teacher and Parent Practices for Children with Autism and Other Developmental Disabilities." *Early Childhood Education Journal* 38(6): 411–20.

McWilliam, R. A., and Stacy Scott. 2001. "A Support Approach to Early Intervention: A Three-Part Framework." *Infants & Young Children* 13(4): 55–66.

Militerni, Roberto, Carmela Bravaccio, Carmelinda Falco, Cinzia Fico, and Mark T. Palermo. 2002. "Repetitive Behaviors in Autistic Disorder." *European Child & Adolescent Psychiatry* 11(5): 210–18.

Milley, Allison, and Wendy Machalicek. 2012. "Decreasing Students' Reliance on Adults: A Strategic Guide for Teachers of Students with Autism Spectrum Disorders." *Intervention in School and Clinic* 48: 66–75.

Minshew, Nancy J., and Timothy A. Keller. 2010. "The Nature of Brain Dysfunction in Autism: Functional Brain Imaging Studies." *Current Opinion in Neurology* 23(2): 124–30.

Morrow, Barry, and Ronald Bass (screenplay). 1988. *Rain Man*. Directed by Barry Levinson. Beverly Hills, CA: United Artists.

National Staff Development Council. 2001. National Staff Development Council's Standards for Staff Development. http://www.gtlcenter.org/sites/default /files/docs/pa/3_PDPartnershipsandStandards /NSDCStandards_No.pdf

Notbohm, Ellen. 2012. *Ten Things Every Child with Autism Wishes You Knew*. Arlington, TX: Future Horizons.

Ozonoff, Sally, and David L. Strayer. 1997. "Inhibitory Function in Nonretarded Children with Autism." *Journal of Autism and Developmental Disorders* 27(1): 59–77.

Porter, Noriko. 2012. "Promotion of Pretend Play for Children with High-Functioning Autism Through the Use of Circumscribed Interests." *Early Childhood Education Journal* 40(3): 161–67.

Rogers, Sally J., Geraldine Dawson, and Laurie A. Vismara. 2012. *An Early Start for Your Child with Autism: Using Everyday Activities to Help Kids Connect, Communicate, and Learn.* New York, NY: Guilford Press.

Saulnier, Cynthia A., and Pamela E. Venntola. 2012. *Essentials of Autism Spectrum Disorders Evaluation and Assessment.* Hoboken, NJ: Wiley.

Schmit, Janet, Sandra Alper, Donna Raschke, and Diane Ryndak. 2000. "Effects of Using a Photographic Cueing Package During Routine School Transitions with a Child Who Has Autism." *Mental Retardation* 38: 131–37.

Sheehey, Patricia, and Patrick Sheehey. 2007. "Elements for Successful Parent-Professional Collaboration: The Fundamental Things Apply as Time Goes By." Teaching Exceptional *Children Plus* (4)2: 1–12.

Sicile-Kira, Chantal. 2004. *Autism Spectrum Disorders: The Complete Guide to Understanding Autism, Asperger's Syndrome, Pervasive Developmental Disorder, and Other ASDs*. New York: Berkley.

Staehr, Lars Stenius. 2008. "Vocabulary Size and the Skills of Listening, Reading and Writing." *Language Learning Journal* 36(2): 139–52.

Stickles Goods, Kelly, Eric Ishijima, Ya-Chih Chang, and Connie Kasari. 2013. "Preschool Based JASPER Intervention in Minimally Verbal Children with Autism: Pilot RCT." *Journal of Autism and Developmental Disorders* 43(5): 1050–56.

Thousand, Jacqueline S., and Richard A. Villa. 2000. *Collaborative Teams: A Powerful Tool in School Restructuring.* Baltimore, MD: Brookes.

Treffert, Darold A. 2009. "The Savant Syndrome: An Extraordinary Condition. A Synopsis: Past, Present, Future." *Philosophical Transactions of the Royal Society B: Biological Sciences* 364(1522): 1351–57.

U.S. Department of Education, National Center for Education Statistics. 2013. "Fast Facts." *Digest of Education Statistics,* accessed September 1, 2015. http://nces.ed.gov/fastfacts/display.asp?id=59

Vedora, Joseph, Robert Ross, and Kelly Kelm. 2008. "Feeding Frenzy: Using Picture Schedules to Reduce Mealtime Struggles." *Teaching Exceptional Children Plus* 4(6): 2–11.

Wadsworth, Danielle D., Leah E. Robinson, Karen Beckham, and Kip Webster. 2012. "Break for Physical Activity: Incorporating Classroom-Based Physical Activity Breaks into Preschools." *Early Childhood Education Journal* 39(6): 391–95.

Wang, Caroline, and Mary Ann Burris. 1997. "Photovoice: Concept, Methodology, and Use for Participatory Needs Assessment." *Health Education & Behavior* 24(3): 369–87.

Wilson, Kaitlyn P. 2012. "Coaching in Early Education Classrooms Serving Children with Autism: A Pilot Study." *Early Childhood Education Journal* 40(2): 97–105.

Wing, Lorna, and Judith Gould. 1979. "Severe Impairments of Social Interaction and Associated Abnormalities in Children: Epidemiology and Classification." *Journal of Autism and Developmental Disorders* 9(1): 11–29.

Index